"This book is a rare gift to those of us who long to live lives that are pleasing to God and yet struggle to know how to do that on a daily basis. Leslie calls us back to a life lived in vulnerable honesty with ourselves, with God, and our world. The truth will indeed set us free."

—SHEILA WALSH
Author, speaker, and vocalist

"This book will add some 'Super Bloom' to the roots of your spiritual life! Leslie Vernick, with solid biblical and personal examples, encourages readers to make an active plan to live out their faith. *The TRUTH Principle* has great potential to help people apply a deep change of heart to everyday life."

—JOHN TRENT, PH.D.
President, Encouraging Words
and Strongfamilies.com

"Leslie Vernick masterfully blends timeless biblical truths with fresh insights and practical applications. *The TRUTH Principle* will bless all who seek transformed minds and hearts."

—SANDRA D. WILSON, PH.D.
Visiting Professor at Trinity Evangelical Seminary
Author of *Released from Shame*

"*The TRUTH Principle* is a must-read for Christian workers leading counseling and discipleship ministries in their churches. Its practical-but-biblical, simple-but-profound approach to understanding our human problems and using them to help us change and grow spiritually is a refreshing alternative to the flood of pop psychology's self-help literature."

—KEVIN D. HUGGINS, PH.D.
Author of *Parenting Adolescents*
Professor of Christian Counseling
Philadelphia College of Bible Graduate School

"With warmth and a therapist's insight, Leslie Vernick gently urges the reader to face tough but life-changing truth. She guides the reader through a workable and practical program for individual growth and change, while also inspiring with penetrating insight."

—GARY THOMAS
Adjunct Faculty at Western Seminary, Portland, Oregon
Author of *Sacred Marriage: Celebrating Marriage As a Spiritual Discipline*

"Leslie Vernick's writing style is that of a sensitive counselor and teacher. She uses biblical truth as a basis for her TRUTH Principle and illustrates each of the steps so readers can conceptualize how to use the principle in their lives. As a teacher, I see this book as a practical and productive teaching tool."

—DR. DONALD L. MacCULLOUGH
Senior Vice President for Academics
Philadelphia College of Bible Graduate School

"Leslie not only affirms that embracing truth is the gateway to personal and spiritual maturity, she lays out in a clear, practical manner how we can embrace truth in dealing with life issues. A wealth of stories vividly illustrates the basic principles of the model. The result is a book that will be enormously helpful for anyone willing to hear and embrace the message."

—GLEN SHELLRUDE, PH.D.
Academic Dean at Alliance Biblical Seminary
Manila, Philippines

"This book works. It is not a quick fix that offers superficial and temporary solutions. It is a practical guide to genuine change that comes from the heart. This book also makes us work. But, somehow, with Leslie's gracious, wise, and personal tutelage, it seems like a wonderful hike with a good friend."

—ED WELCH
Director of Counseling, The Christian Counseling and Education Foundation
Author of *When People Are Big and God Is Small*

the

TRUTH

Principle

the
TRUTH
Principle

A Life-Changing Model for
Spiritual Growth and Renewal

LESLIE VERNICK

WATERBROOK
PRESS

THE TRUTH PRINCIPLE
PUBLISHED BY WATERBROOK PRESS
12265 Oracle Boulevard, Suite 200
Colorado Springs, Colorado 80921

All scripture quotations, unless otherwise indicated, are taken from the *Holy Bible, New International Version®*. NIV® Copyright © 1973, 1978, 1984 by the International Bible Society. Used by permission of Zondervan Publishing House. All rights reserved. Scripture quotations marked (KJV) are taken from the *King James Version*. Scripture quotations marked (MSG) are taken from *The Message*. Copyright © by Eugene H. Peterson 1993, 1994, 1995. Used by permission of NavPress Publishing Group. Scripture quotations marked (NEB) are taken from *The New English Bible* copyright © 1961, 1970 by the Delegates of the Oxford University Press and the Syndics of the Cambridge University Press.

ISBN 978-1-57856-231-2

Published in the United States by WaterBrook Multnomah, an imprint of the Crown Publishing Group, a division of Random House Inc., New York.

WATERBROOK and its deer colophon are registered trademarks of Random House Inc.

Library of Congress Cataloging-in-Publication Data
Vernick, Leslie.
    The TRUTH principle : a life-changing model for spiritual growth and renewal / Leslie Vernick.—1st ed.
        p. cm.
    Includes bibliographical references.
    ISBN 1-57856-231-7
    1. Christian life. 2. Change—Religious aspects—Christianity. I. Title.
BV4501.2.V415 2000
248.4—dc21

                                                                    99-049838

146620572

To my parents

RICHARD AND ALICE BERG

CONTENTS

ACKNOWLEDGMENTS

The author of a book is only one part of the story. In my case, many helpers, wise mentors, encouragers, and friends have prayed for me and contributed to my personal and professional development and my love for God over the years. Without their influence, this book would not have been possible.

Thanks, Dad, for demonstrating *hesed,* or "faithful love," to me. You taught me not to give up and pursued me because I was your daughter, in spite of my rebellion. Mom, thank you for showing me *agape,* or "unconditional love." I was quite unlovable during my early teenage years, yet your steadfastness, which came from your love for God, impacted my soul, and I am forever grateful.

Howard, you believed I could do it long before I even thought I might write a book. Your love and affirmation has ministered healing to me throughout our twenty-five years together. You not only picked up the slack when I was under pressure to meet deadlines, but you never complained either. Ryan and Amanda, you, too, have been encouraging and patient, especially when it looked like Christmas 1998 might be far less than our usual family traditions and celebrations. Thank you.

Theresa Cain, bless you for faithfully praying for me, my ministry, and my family over the years. You are indeed a kindred spirit and a wonderful friend. A special thank-you to Dave and Barb Schindler. You were most kind in letting me use your beach house where I could think, pray, and write.

To my teachers and mentors from the Christian Counseling and Educational Foundation (CCEF): a big thank-you for teaching me to think biblically and to train myself to always look at life from God's point of view. I am indebted to you for challenging me and encouraging me to stick to truth. A special thanks to Ed Welch from CCEF, Lowell Hoffman, Glenna Dameron, and Georgia Shaffer for taking time out of your busy schedules to read through the first draft of my manuscript and for offering me constructive feedback and help. You all were immensely encouraging throughout the writing process.

I'd also like to thank my counselors' support group, especially Sue Reilley, Christopher Zang, Glenna Dameron, and Sandy Plummer. Without your support and fervent prayers, this dream would never have become a reality. I am also so grateful to CLASS (Christian Leaders and Speakers Services) for introducing me to the publishing world and for generously sharing your wisdom with me.

So many of my clients have enriched my life and taught me to walk in truth. Your commitment to finding God in the midst of your pain has been an inspiration to me. Thank you for allowing me to be a part of your journey.

To Erin Healy, my editor: Thanks for your constructive feedback, great encouragement, and light touch. You turned an intimidating process into something I would never have imagined could actually be enjoyable.

And with my whole heart, Lord, I am grateful to you for planting this book in my mind, working it through in my heart, and gently bringing it to fruition.

INTRODUCTION

I have no greater joy than to hear that my children are
walking in the truth.

3 JOHN 4

For a long time into my Christian experience, I didn't know how to walk in the truth. Periodically I would recommit to trying harder, but my efforts were never consistent. I knew what the truth was and how it was supposed to change me, but I got sidetracked trying to live the Christian life without deeply cultivating my relationship with the One who *is* Truth.

When we become Christians, Jesus gives us the privilege of becoming a part of his family, as well as the opportunity to develop our true self and to experience life in a whole new way. I'm afraid, however, that deep in the hearts of many who come to Christ for salvation, nothing much changes. We still struggle with the same sins, the same problems, the same fears, and the same hurts. Sometimes spending time with God seems more like an obligation, a chore, something to check off our to-do list rather than a time to refresh and nourish our soul.

After eighteen years of counseling hurting Christians, I have found that many become weary along the road toward maturity. Some go through cycles of giving up, living it up, and then, when under conviction, trying harder. But change never seems to last very long. Others haven't grasped the idea that becoming a Christian should impact the way they think, feel, and act. These people love the theology of "once saved always saved" but are oblivious to the harder sayings of Jesus, which tell us that if we love him we will obey his commandments. I asked one man whom I was counseling what his relationship with Jesus was like. He said, "I got saved when I was a boy, and that's all I need." When I pressed to see whether there was anything more to his Christian life, he looked at me with a blank expression and said, "My parents taught me the right way to believe, and I believe it."

Unlike this man, many of us are searching for a deeper and closer relationship with Christ. We long for the intimacy that the psalmist David shared with God. We desire the changed life of the apostle Paul and the power of the Holy Spirit working in us. We are not content merely knowing the right things to believe; instead, we want to see them worked out in our life in practical and real ways. We wonder why we don't bear spiritual fruit, or how we can participate more fully with God in the process of reaching maturity.

Despite the abundant availability of both self-help books and Bible-study materials, many of us find it difficult to apply what we learn and make that long head-to-heart journey of change. When our responses to life's daily trials lack the Christian maturity we desire, we see with frustrating clarity just how far we have to go. Is it possible to achieve a deeper, more permanent change of heart?

Yes. Woven throughout this book is a practical, simple-to-understand and easy-to-remember model for spiritual growth called the TRUTH Principle. This simple acronym will help us remember specific steps to take toward maturity. It teaches us how to walk in the truth by deepening our relationship with Jesus through learning to practice his presence. Each step of the TRUTH Principle is illustrated with specific teaching and application for a more intimate relationship with Christ and a more permanent (although not perfect) change of heart. As you apply it to your life each day you will:

- Gain a new perspective on the *Troubles* God allows in your life.
- Come to better understand your *Response* to those trials.
- Discover the *Underlying idols* that hamper your efforts to change.
- Learn how to discern the *Truth* of God's Word.
- Begin to develop a *Heart response* that will draw you closer to God.

I, too, am on the path of Christian maturity. I have not arrived but am in the process of walking in the truth and practicing the presence of God. Throughout this journey, God desires to make us partakers in his divine nature (Hebrews 12:10)—to make us more like Jesus.

Jesus said, "You will know the truth, and the truth will set you free" (John 8:32). Jesus *is* the Truth. Knowing him sets us free. Free from what? Free from ourselves—the bondage to the old man, the false self, the person we have created. Then we are free to become our true self, born in the likeness of God. The TRUTH Principle describes a process of "walking in the truth," of being restored to God's image in us. It comes about through our union and relationship with the One who is Truth and Love.

Transformation! That is what is promised for those of us who say we know God. Transformation—not just of our head, but of our whole heart. And this change begins by knowing God.

PART I

What Moves Our Heart to Change Our Ways?

CHAPTER ONE

RULES DON'T CHANGE US— CHANGE US— RELATIONSHIPS DO

*MY GOD, Thou has helped me to see…that blessedness
does not lie so much in receiving good from and in thee,
but in holding forth thy glory and virtue: that it is an
amazing thing to see Deity in a creature, speaking, acting,
filling, shining through it; that nothing is good but thee,
that I am near good when I am near thee, that to be like
thee is a glorious thing: This is my magnet, my attraction.*

VALLEY OF VISION

When I was fourteen, my life radically changed. Until then I lived in Chicago. I was the oldest of three children, and we lived with our mother in a tiny one-bedroom apartment on the north side. I slept on the couch; my siblings slept on the floor.

Mom was an alcoholic and had many emotional problems. She gave us little supervision. At fourteen I thought that was great. I could do whatever I wanted. I had no one telling me what to do, no rules other than "Don't get in Mom's way."

Then the unthinkable happened. My father was awarded custody of us. After my parents' divorce, he recommitted his life to Christ, remarried, and moved to the Chicago suburbs. He knew of my mother's behavior and had been petitioning the court for years to get custody but had never won. This time he did.

I had to move, and at his home there were rules. Lots of rules. We could not go to movies or dances. We could not play cards. We had to attend church two times on Sunday and once during the week. We had to go to school regularly and do our homework. We had chores to do and could not use the phone whenever we wanted.

There were other rules, but I can't recall all of them. What I do remember is being angry—very angry—and having a heart that was as warm as a stone in Alaska. I didn't like all the rules, and I especially didn't like having this God business shoved at me.

But I remember something else, too. My father and stepmother were patient with me. They understood that I was experiencing a radical change. I remember my outbursts, and their kindness when I deserved punishment. I remember my stepmother taking me shopping for new school clothes after I arrived with nothing but the clothes on my back. I remember getting three meals a day (something I don't ever remember getting before) and even regular snacks.

I remember their prayers, and most of all I remember their love, which began to dismantle the brick wall I had built around my heart. It was their love, not their rules, that began to affect my life. Yes, the rules helped to provide me with some structure, but my heart was not responsive to the rules. It was responsive to the love that was behind them.

Has anyone ever significantly influenced your life? Caused you to change direction? Perhaps a teacher, coach, good friend, mentor? Maybe your spouse or even your parents? If so, this is how it should be.

God has made us relational beings, and we are significantly affected and changed by our close interpersonal relationships.

Psychologists and counselors have known for years that the most important ingredient for successful therapy is a good relationship. Study after study confirms that many different therapeutic models can be effective in counseling someone, but without a good relationship the client cannot be helped. As a counselor, I might have great skills and all the information necessary to help someone, but if that person doesn't trust me or can't relate to me, I will never impact his life in a positive way.

I'm afraid that we Christians sometimes lose our way toward spiritual maturity because we focus more on the rules of the faith than on our relationship with Jesus. We understand Christianity as "contractual instead of personal."[1] We think that if we confess our sins we get forgiveness and eternal life. We do, but Jesus offers us far more than forgiveness. We now have a personal and intimate relationship with him in which he calls us his family and his friends.

For a long time I was content with being saved and making sure that my doctrine was correct. My devotions, when I had them, consisted of reading the Bible and looking for what I was supposed to do or obey. I did not know God deeply or intimately. When I was honest with myself, I had to admit I didn't experience the joy of the Lord or God speaking to my innermost heart, which I'd heard other Christians speak of. I knew the right things to believe, and I "believed" them, but my belief never resulted in any significant change of heart. I was the same person, struggling over and over again with the same sins.

Over the years I have learned that being saved is much more than getting a ticket to heaven. Jesus explained this when he said, "This *is* eternal life: that they may *know* you, the only true God, and Jesus

Christ, whom you have sent" (John 17:3, italics mine). Knowing God starts now and lasts throughout eternity. We will never know him completely because he is infinite. But knowing God will change us, for we cannot encounter the eternal I AM and remain the same.

In my journey to know God I have taken many paths that I thought would lead to deeper intimacy with him. As a young Christian in my late teens and early twenties, much like a young child with her parents, I related to God mostly by asking him for things. I prayed for good things to happen and bad things to stop happening. As I matured, I asked God for more spiritual things. I wanted the fruit of the Spirit and the gifts of the Holy Spirit. Then I wanted experiences with God. I wanted to see miracles. I wanted to feel the Holy Spirit's power in my life. Throughout this journey, my prayers consisted of one-way conversations. I talked to God, telling him what I wanted and needed, but I didn't take the time to listen to him, to allow him to reveal his heart to me.

Recently God showed me this through my son, who was away at college. During a typical phone conversation, Ryan was making requests for money and other needs when he suddenly stopped and asked, "Mom, how are you doing?" I nearly dropped the phone. His question marked a radical change in our relationship. I was no longer a parent who just provided for my child's needs; I was a person in a relationship with another person who cared about me. It felt really good.

These days my prayers have changed. I no longer think of prayer as presenting my list of needs or wants to God and then waiting for him to respond with a yes or no. I no longer pray for special spiritual experiences (although I would be thrilled to have them). More than anything else, I want to know the person of God. Beyond enjoying his gifts, I want to know the giver. As the apostle Paul prayed, "I want to know Christ" (Philippians 3:10). My prayer life has turned away from getting answers from God toward knowing God.

But how? What does it take to know him, to have an intimate walk with him?

KNOWING GOD INVOLVES TALKING WITH AND LISTENING TO GOD

Knowing God intimately involves a relationship where there is a communion of persons. The patriarch Abraham did this through dialogue. So did Moses, Jacob, David, Elijah, Paul, Peter, and Jesus. We are creatures of conversation; that is the way we get to know someone. We build relationships through intimate dialogue.

It is difficult to feel close to someone if no meaningful conversation takes place between you. Some couples come to me for counseling because one spouse "doesn't talk" and the other is unhappy about it. If the two do talk, it's primarily about what's for dinner, who needs to take the kids to piano lessons, or whether one could pick up the clothes from the cleaners.

Our conversations with God can also be superficial. We don't share our true heart with him, nor do we listen for his. Sometimes our prayers are nothing more than asking God to do this or that for us. The Bible describes Moses, one of God's closest friends, as knowing the ways of God, whereas Israel (who had a more superficial relationship with God) just looked for God's deeds (Psalm 103:7). Oswald Chambers says that "the idea of prayer is not in order to get answers from God; prayer is perfect and complete oneness with God."[2]

Communion, expressed through intimate dialogue, is the heart's way of knowing God better. Did you ever notice in Genesis that Abraham asked God many questions? What are your heart's questions for God? Prayer is a dialogue, not a monologue. When you ask him your heart's questions, do you wait for an answer?

If you're anything like me, you hate to wait. We take books in the car so if we get stuck in traffic we won't get bored. We get aggravated waiting in line, waiting on the phone, waiting for a tardy friend. Waiting on God, for his timing, is also hard for us. In our fast-paced lives, waiting seems like such a waste of our valuable time. But it is often in the labor of waiting that trust is born.

Oswald Chambers said that a mark of truly intimate friends is that they will confide not their sorrows, but their secret joys.[3] Do you know what the secret joys of God are? During your time of prayer do you cup your ear to the heart of God, or do you just want to unload yours?

KNOWING GOD INVOLVES LEARNING TO DISCERN GOD'S VOICE

Listening is hard work for us. Most of us spend far more time talking than carefully listening to people. The next time you are in a conversation with your spouse or friend, ask yourself, "Did I focus all my attention on listening attentively, or was I thinking ahead to my next sentence, or was I distracted by other things I need to do?" When Ryan was a small child and I wasn't listening carefully to him, he would grab my cheeks between his chubby hands and come in close, nose-to-nose, and say, "Mommy, you have to listen to me now!"

If simple listening is difficult, listening for God's voice is even harder. We often find ourselves paying more attention to the competing voices of the world, the flesh, and the devil. All vie for our ear. Sometimes it seems their volume is pitched much higher than God's. We have to learn how to tune out the competing voices and to listen for God's still, small voice.

As children, many of us played that game in which we were blindfolded, spun around three times, and then pointed toward a destination that we had to reach while still blindfolded. The voices of the crowd shouted which way to go.

"Move to your right," yelled one voice.

Another shouted, "No! Stop—make a sharp left." Some of the voices purposely tried to distract and confuse the blindfolded person from reaching her goal. Usually one loyal friend in the crowd tried to give more accurate directions. Sooner or later the blindfolded person had to decide which voice to trust and which distracting voices to tune out. Unseeing, she inched toward her destination, hoping she wouldn't go astray. When the blindfold was removed, she found out if she'd trusted the right voice.

Terry,[4] a former client of mine, struggled daily with feelings of inferiority and self-doubt. These feelings constantly plagued her, even as a Christian. Her internal voices taunted her with thoughts that people would not really want to be her friend, that she was not useful to God's work, and that she didn't have anything of value to offer others. These voices of self-doubt and inferiority often seemed much louder and stronger to her than the voice of her heavenly Father, who always seeks to reassure her of her value and his love. But as she grew more and more familiar with the sound of his voice whispering words of truth to her, she began to stand straighter, and those taunting voices started to lose their power over her life.

Jesus tells us, "My sheep listen to my voice" (John 10:27). What does the voice of God sound like to you? Is it harsh and condemning? Is it a voice that says, "Good try, but you'll never measure up"? Sometimes we confuse the voice of God with our own internal voices (our flesh) or even that of our accuser—the deceiver Satan. For Terry, her internal voices taunted her about her shortcomings and lied to her about her value and worth. For a while, she thought she was hearing God's voice expressing anger and displeasure toward her. As she deepened her relationship with God, she realized that the taunting and critical voices inside her head were not from God. The next step for Terry was to choose not to listen to or believe those voices so that she would not be led astray.

Unlike Terry, John patted himself on the back and told himself that God must be pretty pleased with him. After all, he was doing so many great things for Christ's kingdom. This was not God's voice, however, but the voice of self-righteousness.

Another familiar voice is that of self-pity. It sounds something like this: "You've had a rough day (or rough life). No one understands how difficult it is for you. How could you be expected to mature or obey God? It's not fair!"

The voice of self-indulgence is another frequent companion. It tells us, "You deserve to be happy. Go ahead—it won't hurt anyone." And most of us recognize the tyrannical voice of self-condemnation: "You miserable failure! You really blew it. Who do you think you are?"

Don't be misled. These voices are not God's voice. Deepening our relationship with him involves coming to recognize his voice and learning to tune out the ones that distract and lie to us. Studying the gospels and meditating on Jesus' voice teaches us what God's voice is like, for the Bible tells us that Jesus is the exact representation of the nature of God (Hebrews 1:3). In this way we can know what the voice of God sounds like. It is totally truthful and always for our good. It is loving, kind, pure, correcting, comforting, convicting, instructive, encouraging, and healing. God speaks to us through his Word, his Spirit, and his people. As he speaks to us, he reveals our heart's true motivations, attitudes, beliefs, and feelings and lovingly prompts us toward action.

I'll never forget a particular time when I experienced God's voice speaking to me in a powerful way. I was preparing for a trip to Manila, in the Philippines, to teach counselors and teachers some specific counseling skills. I had never been out of the United States before except for a vacation to Cancun, and now I was about to travel across the world by myself. I was anxious—terrified, to be exact. I felt inadequate and overwhelmed. My internal voices chattered nonstop that I was not competent to teach and that I was spiritually unprepared for such a great undertaking. I also heard the voice of the enemy, who sought to remind me in detail of all my faults and sins.

I remember standing in front of my copier, sobbing. "I can't go, God. Pick someone else for the job." It was in the midst of this internal storm that God broke through with his beam of light and truth. He reminded my spirit that he would always be with me (Deuteronomy 31:6). He also reminded me that I was indeed inadequate for the task at hand, just as Paul had said he was inadequate in 2 Corinthians 3, but my adequacy would come from God. He told me that this trip would be an opportunity for me to depend on and trust him. As his still, small voice penetrated my heart with truth, I felt renewed with strength. I dried my eyes and was able to step out in faith, believing and trusting God more deeply than I ever had before.

INTIMACY WITH GOD INVOLVES
VALUING WHAT HE SAYS

A couple was squabbling in my office. "He never listens to what I say," she cried.

"I heard exactly what she said," he retorted. "I just don't think it's very important!"

Those simple statements revealed much about the quality of their relationship. *No wonder they're here for counseling,* I thought. *They need a lot of work.*

We can never experience God in a deeper way if we don't value and believe what he tells us. Listening to God involves more than acknowledging what he says. We must value what he says and think it important. We must tuck it deep in our heart and believe it.

Like Terry, who struggled with feelings of inferiority and self-doubt even though she professed to know God's love, many of us experience inner turmoil when our feelings are in opposition to what God tells us. The Bible sometimes strikes us as nothing more than empty words. We don't value what he says. Ultimately, we don't really believe him. We have a head knowledge but not a heart faith. We live by the "truth" of our subjective feelings instead of by the truth of God's Word.

Christian counselor Sandra Wilson says, "We don't always live what we profess, but we always live what we believe."[5] This describes the experience of many when they say, "I know it in my head but not in my heart." We will always live according to what our heart believes, not what our head professes to believe. One of the most difficult journeys a Christian will ever take is the journey from the head to the heart, or from knowledge to trust.

Betty sat in my office, tears streaming down her face. "I just don't feel forgiven," she sobbed. "After what I've done, I can't believe that God would forgive and love me."

Betty professed to be a Christian, but in her heart she believed that the sin she had committed was so bad it was unforgivable. Although her head knew Jesus died to forgive sins, her heart didn't trust that. What she really believed was that God was uninterested in forgiving her sin or unable to forgive it. Her heart's belief that she was unforgivable and that God was uninterested in her overruled her head knowledge of forgiveness, and consequently she could not live a life that felt forgiven.

When your feelings or thoughts are in competition with the voice of God, which wins? Do you value what God says and believe it? Not just in your head but also in your heart? Psalm 119 is filled with the commitment of the psalmist to trust and believe God even in difficult circumstances. God loves it when we believe him, and our relationship grows deeper when we value what he says and obey him. Only when we allow faith and trust to permeate our inner life can our outer life begin to change.

WALKING WITH GOD INTIMATELY MUST INCLUDE OBEYING HIM

God desires us to know him. Knowing God involves hearing him, listening to him, believing him, and obeying him. Sometimes we think that obeying God means gritting our teeth and following the rules. But Jesus doesn't desire external conformity or an intellectual commitment to orthodoxy any more than a parent desires robotic children. He desires us to love him and trust him by willingly yielding our will to his. Obeying God always results in our greatest good and his greatest glory. By contrast, "the person who wants to know God but who has no heart to *obey* God will never enter into the sacred courts where God reveals Himself to the soul of man. God does not give divine knowledge to those who have no desire to glorify Him."[6]

Jesus tells us in John 14:21 that when we obey him, we show our love toward him. Jesus promises that God will make himself more known to us as we commit ourselves to this process. No one drifts into intimacy with another person. It requires time, commitment, and sometimes plain hard work. Would you feel close to someone if he didn't respect what you said? If she didn't believe you, or care about what was important to you, or trust you? God will not disclose himself to those who are not interested in the things that he is interested in or who are not willing to trust and follow his voice.

INTIMACY WITH GOD INVOLVES LOVING HIM WITH OUR WHOLE HEART

Rules won't change us, but a growing relationship with Christ will. Change or maturity for a Christian comes about through deepening our intimacy with Jesus, not by following certain rules or doctrines. When we begin to grasp his love for us, our hearts respond with love for him. He tells us that if we love him, we will keep his commandments (John 14:15). Our love for him is what begins to move our heart toward obedience.

In his book *Seeking the Face of God,* Gary Thomas says, "We cease from sin, not just because we're disciplined, but because we have found something better."[7] We cease when we come to love something else more than ourselves or our sin.

Jesus asked Peter three times if he loved him (John 21:15-17). Why? Because he knew that without loving him, Peter would never change and be the man God designed him to be. Being in a love relationship with Jesus—not adhering to a certain religious belief or doctrine—is what changes our heart.

Remember Matthew the tax collector? What did he love? He loved money, power, prestige. When he met Jesus, something in Matthew's heart changed. He did not love money the most any longer. He loved Jesus the most, and it radically changed the way Matthew handled his money. What did he do? He paid back everyone whom he had swindled.

The woman at the well loved men. Many men. But when she met up with Jesus she experienced what real love was and realized no man's love could substitute for God's love. She was transformed. What happened? Her heart fell in love with something more than the attention of men. Her heart loved Jesus, and that changed her life entirely.

A man named Saul loved the Law. His love for it drove him to zealous persecution of Christians. Then a blinding light met him on his way to Damascus, and Saul had a radical change of heart. He didn't stop loving the Law, but he loved something else *more*, and it made all the difference in the way he interpreted the Law. Even his name changed—he became Paul.

On the other hand, the Pharisees loved being right. They loved having authority and being experts in the technicalities of the Law. But their hearts were cold, their lives brittle. Jesus described them as whitewashed tombs—dead inside. Jesus said, "These people honor me with their lips, but their hearts are far from me. They worship me in vain; their teachings are but rules taught by men" (Matthew 15:8-9). They were so focused on rules that they missed the relationship Christ offered them.

We can only love God to the extent that we know and believe the love he has for us. My good friend Georgia from York, Pennsylvania, told me that during her bone-marrow transplant for breast cancer she had a very clear image of herself being drawn into the arms of Jesus, of being carried by him when she was too weak to walk on her own. She describes deeply experiencing his love and care for her, and responding in her heart with an overwhelming sense of gratitude for his special, tender love. The Scriptures teach us that we love him as a response, because he first loved us (1 John 4:19). It is this union, our abiding in him and he in us, where change begins to take place in our innermost being: our heart. This is where we begin to take on the character of the one we love—Christ's nature in us.

LOVING GOD CHANGES US FROM THE INSIDE OUT

The process of personal growth, Christian maturity, fruitfulness, and becoming more and more like Christ begins with seeds of love sown in our heart. Christ often used the metaphor of garden life as a teaching tool. An apple tree cannot bear figs, can it? Why not? Because the very essence of the apple tree is defined by its roots, which are apple-tree roots and not fig-tree roots. Apples are a natural outgrowth of the roots. We will never have Christlikeness or the fruit of the Spirit in our lives if our roots are shallow, underdeveloped, diseased, or of a different stock.

What are the roots of Christian living? The roots are love. Jesus tells us that we cannot bear fruit unless we are rooted in him (John 15). Just as a branch is in essence and nature like the vine from which it sprouts, we are to reflect God's image in us, and God is love. He tells us that when we love him we will obey him. Rules don't bring heart obedience, but love does.

Paul prays in Ephesians 3 "that you, being rooted and established in love, may have power, together with all the saints, to grasp how wide and long and high and deep is the love of Christ, and to know this love that surpasses knowledge—that you may be filled to the measure of all the fullness of God" (vv. 17-19). In the physical world, fruit and flowers are a natural outgrowth of strong, solid roots. As Christians, we will never develop any spiritual fruit without being rooted and grounded in love, both the love *of* God and the love *for* God. As in nature, the healthier the roots, the more abundant the fruit. I'm afraid that as Christians we have spent too much time trying to cultivate the fruit of the Spirit in our lives and not enough paying attention to the roots.

This change of heart and life for a Christian is a permanent change, but this does not mean that it is a perfect change. When I got married, many things in my life permanently changed. My name changed, my address changed, my sleeping arrangements changed, and my status changed. In addition to these external changes, I began to change internally. I no longer acted like a single woman. Someone else's needs had become at least equally important to me as my own. But I didn't change because I was *supposed* to. I changed because I loved my husband and wanted to please him. Marriage was an outward commitment of the love within my heart.

There are times, especially when I'm angry or hurt, when I think only of myself and not of my husband. On these occasions I act like a selfish person, but I never act like a single person. Change in me has taken place over our twenty-five years of marriage because of the love we share and our special relationship. My commitment to love my husband even when it is hard is based on an act of my will rather than on an emotion or feeling. Thus it is with God. In our relationship with him we experience moments of intense emotional closeness where God seems so real that we are quite sure nothing at all matters in life except that moment of closeness to him. At other times we walk by faith and commitment, regardless of what our feelings tell us at the moment.

Mother Teresa's life was summed up by love. Her love for Jesus changed her—and it radiated in and through her. She often said, "I don't do great things, I do little things with great love."[8] Her dying words were, "Jesus, I love you. Jesus, I love you."[9]

Though this book is about change, change can never be our goal. If it is, we will lose our way. Our relationship with Jesus must always be the starting place and ending place of our heart's transformation. The TRUTH Principle gives us a tool to help us remember the most important commandment of all: "Love the LORD your God with all your heart and with all your soul and with all your strength" (Deuteronomy 6:5).

God longs for people to desire and seek a personal and intimate relationship with him above all else. When life is going smoothly we often forget him. At times he interrupts our life to get our attention and to remind us what is important and true. In order to grow up into maturity and become more like Jesus, we must begin by seeing what God is up to during the more difficult times and understanding our troubles from his perspective.

TIME FOR REFLECTION

1. If God told you today that he would grant you the deepest desire of your heart, what would you ask him for? In order to gain the most

from this question, take the time to answer it now, before you continue reading.

What you asked God for reveals what you think you need the most. If you could ask only one thing of God and be sure he would grant it, would you ask to know him better? As Christians, God says that is what we need the most. Read Philippians 3:7-16. Pray with Paul that you would consider all things unimportant in comparison to knowing Christ. This is where the journey of the heart begins.

2. Honestly evaluate your relationship with God over the past six months. Is it growing deeper and closer? Are you loving him with all your heart, all your mind, and all your strength? This is what God longs for from you. What hinders this relationship for you? What voices do you listen to other than God's? What steps could you begin to take this week to deepen your intimacy with God?

3. Consider beginning a prayer journal as you work your way through this book. During prayer, write down any thoughts, verses, songs, or impressions that come to your mind. After reading God's Word and listening for his voice, ask yourself, "Do I believe what God has said? Do I not only acknowledge it with my mind but also trust it with my heart?"

PART II

The TRUTH
Principle

CHAPTER TWO

TROUBLES AND TRIALS: THE LATHE THAT SHAPES OUR HEARTS

*Consider it pure joy, my brothers, whenever you face tri-
als of many kinds, because you know that the testing of
your faith develops perseverance. Perseverance must finish its work so that you may be mature and complete,
not lacking anything.*

JAMES 1:2-4

While pregnant with my first child, I learned that my husband and I
would be unable to have any more children. After Ryan was born, I
was so overwhelmed with thankfulness that I didn't think much about
the future. But when Ryan turned three, my heart ached for another
baby.

At the time, I was volunteering as a counselor at our local Crisis
Pregnancy Center. One day a woman came in for a pregnancy test.
Her test was negative, but she was struggling as a single mother and
needed some extra help. Over the next several months, Sue and I
became friends. One day she asked me why I didn't have more children. I told her my story, and she asked if I had considered adoption.

"Of course," I replied, "but healthy infants are not exactly easy to come by these days."

It just so happened that Sue had a pregnant friend who was seeking an adoptive family for her baby. She was single, forty, and already had four children. *What a perfect situation God has arranged!* I thought. This woman knew what motherhood was. She was not an idealistic teenager. Surely, if she was contemplating adoption, she was serious.

I was elated and grateful to God. He had seen the cry of my heart and answered my longings in a miraculous way. Through Sue, the pregnant woman and I met, and she agreed that my husband and I would be the ones to adopt her baby. She would call me as soon as she went into labor. We could take the baby home right from the hospital. She was due around Christmas—only two months away.

"Isn't God good!" I said again and again, beaming to family and friends. "What a miracle that I would just *happen* to develop this relationship with Sue, who knew this woman who was pregnant. God knew all along that he would bring another baby into our lives." I felt like I could have walked on water.

Christmas came and we eagerly waited for the phone call. None came. A week later, still no call. My heart began to tremble.

"What if she changed her mind and kept the baby?" I cried to my husband. But my rational mind thought that was unlikely. She was pretty definite about not wanting another child. Finally I couldn't wait another minute. I called Sue.

"Sue, I haven't heard anything yet! What's going on?"

Sue paused slightly. "I know. I've been afraid to call you."

My heart dropped straight to my feet, and the room started to spin. Something terrible must have happened to the baby. I whispered, "Did the baby die?"

A long moment later she said, "No, Leslie, he didn't die. He was born two weeks ago, but...um...I don't know how to tell you this. She gave him to someone else to adopt."

"What?" I couldn't believe what I was hearing. I think my heart stopped beating. Sharp pain ripped through my body. I felt like I had exploded into a million pieces. I could have accepted the mother changing her mind, even the baby dying, more easily than I could accept the mother choosing someone else to adopt her baby. How could God allow this to happen? We were supposed to get that baby! I had been deceived, tricked! I had trusted God, and this was what I got? Heart-wrenching pain? I was furious. God was not good! I careened headfirst into a full-blown crisis of faith.

AN ETERNAL PERSPECTIVE

Scott Peck opens his best-selling book *The Road Less Traveled* with the statement "Life is difficult."[1] Everyone can relate. Even for the person who knows God, life is full of troubles. Sometimes the troubles are big, like my failed adoption. The cold wind of adversity can strip us bare and chill us to the very core of our being. More often, however, the little things that invade our day-to-day lives shape our troubles. They are fingernails against a blackboard or pebbles in our shoe, ever-present irritants that capture our attention and make us beg for relief.

Often it is during the times of troubles and trials in our life when we ask God our most penetrating questions: Why, God? Why this? Why me? Why now? I have found that people ask these same questions whether facing big troubles, such as a diagnosis of cancer or the loss of a job or dealing with everyday trials, like being stuck in a traffic jam while trying to keep an important appointment or burning dinner when company is due.

The question *Why?* in its various forms is natural to ask, and many people in both the Old Testament and New Testament asked God this very question when they had troubles. Perhaps we are most familiar with Job. He lost his family, his fortune, and his health. His troubles were devastating. Job didn't understand why God was allowing this. Nor did God ever explain to Job that he was in an eternal battle. Because we humans have limited perspective, like Job we will never completely see the big picture this side of heaven. Many of us (myself included), however, get stuck trying to understand and explain the ways of God. When our plans to adopt fell through, I couldn't conceive of any explanation that made sense. Why would God bring us so close to adopting that baby and then allow him to be snatched from our hands? Years later, I still don't know. Yet in this journey of knowing God and deepening our relationship with him, God doesn't ask us to understand him. Instead, he wants us to trust him.

My parakeet, Sydney, lives his life in a small round cage in my kitchen. He has good food, clean water, a couple of perches, and a bell that he loves to ring. He says "pretty bird" and will kiss the lips of anyone who presses her face next to his cage. Sometimes, though not often, he comes out for a quick flight around the kitchen. But the room's bigness frightens him, so he prefers the security of his perch. He seems happy and sings so loud people often ask me if I have birds. I tell them, "No, only one very loud bird."

Sydney knows nothing of fresh air, beautiful leaves, and tall branches where other birds nest. He has never sipped cool water from a pond or had the fun of hunting worms in the early spring morning. He is small and has a limited perspective of the world. His cage and perhaps the kitchen are all he knows of the world, and for him, it is the only reality there is. But we know this is not all there is to reality. A great big world lies beyond the cage and kitchen that Sydney knows nothing about.

Sometimes God reminds me that Sydney and I are not that different. I am small. I am limited. I am bound by time, space, and my human flesh. I know nothing about eternity or the bigness of God. All I know is what I experience. But my experience does not define the boundaries of reality. No—there is more to it, beyond what I can see or even imagine. Just because I do not know it doesn't make it less real or true. God offers us glimpses into this "true reality" (as I will call it) if we will take the time to see through the lens of his eternal perspective.

WHY? THE REASON FOR TRIALS AND TROUBLES

Job had a few friends who thought they knew why Job's troubles began. They sought to counsel him, sadly adding more grief to Job's already heavy heart.

Sometimes we think we can explain the ways of God to troubled hearts. Like Job's friends, we may presume to know the reason why someone suffers. We say things like "God is disciplining you. There must be some unconfessed sin in your life." Or "If only you prayed harder and had more faith, God would answer you." This kind of remark tends to increase a person's pain; in my adoption situation, had someone said something similar I would have found myself enraged, not comforted!

Although in the following passages I will seek to give biblical answers to help us understand some of the reasons behind life's troubles and how God uses them in our lives, I would offer a caveat: Having answers isn't enough. In a time of suffering, explanations usually do little to ease the pain. Even if God himself had told me why he allowed that baby to be adopted by another couple, it would have done little to comfort me. Answers are helpful but not always comforting. The Lord and his people, not answers, comfort us. We need to be careful when we minister to others not to substitute simplistic answers for real caring. That said, let's consider a few reasons why trouble enters life.

THE ETERNAL BATTLE FOR OUR DEVOTION —WHOM WILL
WE TRUST? WHOM WILL WE LOVE?

In the preface to the story of Job, God gives us a peek behind the eternal curtain into a battle between God and Satan.

> One day the angels came to present themselves before the LORD, and Satan also came with them. The LORD said to Satan, "Where have you come from?"
>
> Satan answered the LORD, "From roaming through the earth and going back and forth in it."
>
> Then the LORD said to Satan. "Have you considered my servant Job? There is no one on earth like him; he is blameless and upright, a man who fears God and shuns evil."
>
> "Does Job fear God for nothing?" Satan replied. "Have you not put a hedge around him and his household and everything he has? You have blessed the work of his hands, so that his flocks and herds are spread throughout the land. But stretch out your hand and strike everything he has, and he will surely curse you to your face." (Job 1:6-11)

The constant taunt of Satan toward God is this: Your people don't love you for you; they just love you because you're good to them. Take that away and they will curse you. God allowed Satan to test Job to prove that wasn't true. Would you pass the test? I didn't when God allowed the adoption to fall through. I was angry and didn't want anything to do with him. He let me down. He failed me. My response to my troubles showed that I didn't love him for who he is, but only for what he could give me. When the adoption didn't happen, I found my faith and my relationship with God inadequate to sustain the overwhelming pain.

Many times throughout our life, our heart will be subject to the same question. Our circumstances may not be as dramatic as Job's, but the bottom line is the same: If you lost everything, would God be enough? When God is silent and doesn't give you the answers you want or relief from your troubles, does your heart still trust him? Do you still love him? Our troubles reveal our understanding of God and test our relationship with him. Is our relationship based on who he is, or is it based on what he does for us? Job committed himself to trust and worship God even when God took everything away.

When my hopes for the baby were dashed, my faith shattered. But at that point God began to slowly rebuild our relationship based on who he is and not on what he gives or doesn't give.

Many people define God according to what happens in their life. When life is full of well-being, good health, and blessings, they say, "Isn't God good?" When the tables are turned and life feeds us bitter herbs, we are tempted to define God accordingly. In those situations we usually don't think of God as good or loving. Rather, we think of God as wrathful, vengeful, unloving, forgetful, distant, uncaring—adjectives that reflect our feelings more than God's nature or character (see Diagram 2.1).[2]

In the third chapter of Lamentations, Jeremiah struggled to identify God's true nature. After serving the Lord faithfully, Jeremiah ended up in a deep pit, having been thrown there by his enemies. He accused God of turning against him and intentionally wounding him. Jeremiah defined God's character through the lens of his circumstances. But later in the same chapter, Jeremiah had a change of heart when he recalled the truth of who God is. Although his circumstances didn't change, Jeremiah now cried, "for his compassions never fail. They are new every morning; great is your faithfulness" (vv. 22-23). Despite circumstantial evidence to the contrary, Jeremiah chose to believe and trust that God is good. Knowing God's character helped Jeremiah bear difficult circumstances and still trust God in the process.

Diagram 2.1

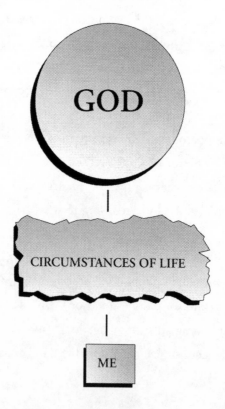

Job, too, asked God, "*Why?* What have I done to deserve this suffering?" Yet Job never questioned God's goodness as I did. Job's heart knew God was in control and sovereign over the affairs of his life. Although Job didn't understand, he chose to trust him. At the end of Job's experience, he proclaimed that although he had heard of God, it wasn't until that moment that he really knew him (Job 42:1-6). Satan lost the battle, and God used this experience in Job's life to deepen his love relationship with Job.

SIN—BOTH OUR OWN AND OTHERS

A second reason for troubles in this life is an obvious one: Sin. Since sin entered the world, mankind has been plagued with troubles, both as the consequences of our own sins and as the result of others' sin. Sometimes we think we can sin and not reap the painful consequences. At times it seems like we do get away with it. But God's Word is clear: Whatever we sow we will reap (Galatians 6:7-8). Unfortunately, during the reaping we are often tempted to blame God. "Why did God let this happen to me?" sobbed a young teenage girl who learned she had contracted genital herpes after being sexually active.

More difficult for many of us is suffering as a result of someone else's sin. When the birth mother betrayed our trust by giving her child to another couple, she went on with her life but left us brokenhearted. How can we believe God loves us when he allows people to sin against us? What do we say to the family whose teenage daughter was killed by a drunk driver or to the mother whose only son was paralyzed by a stray bullet? How about the wife whose husband decides to end their marriage for another woman and leaves the family financially and emotionally devastated? No answer would provide much comfort. Only in our personal relationship with Jesus will we find any comfort during times of suffering, because we know that he, too, suffered because of others' sins. It is difficult to reconcile these truths: God is Love, and he loves us, yet he allows people to sin against those whom he loves and does not always intervene. From the beginning of time, however, God has given people free will. As a result, it would be contrary to God's plan to take away our choice to sin—even when it hurts his children, as it did his very own Son.

A Broken World

Often trials and troubles come from everyday situations that are the result of living in an imperfect world. Earthquakes and tornadoes bring devastation. Appliances and automobiles break down at the most inconvenient times. Accidents that can't be blamed on anyone impact lives forever.

At fifteen, James was good-looking and popular with the girls. During an afternoon of water skiing with friends, he dove into shallow water. That single incident changed his life forever. James broke his neck and now uses a wheelchair and is dependent upon others for the simplest tasks. Why James? Why that?

We cannot control many things, nor even understand why they happen. When we insist upon knowing why as a prerequisite to healing or growth, we lose our way in our journey toward knowing God. Instead of asking why, which limits us to a temporal perspective, a more productive question is to ask, "What is God doing in me through the troubles he allows in my life?" Our troubles become the lathe that God uses to shape our hearts into his image. As we come to know—to *believe*—that God's heart is always good and always loving, we can take great comfort in knowing that he uses *all* the circumstances of our life—those that are good, those that are bad, those that are a result of our own sin or someone else's sin or no one's sin at all—to bring about his good purposes in us.

James is a different person today than he was as an energetic, athletic young man. Today, James radiates the love of Christ and lives for the glory of God, not for his own personal pleasure or happiness. The miracle that God rendered in James's heart as a result of his accident is no less astounding than if God had healed his broken neck and said, "James, get up and walk."

WHAT IS GOD UP TO IN MY LIFE?

God's purposes and will are mysterious to many Christians. We often anguish for days trying to discern what God wants in our life in a particular circumstance. Was it God's will that we adopt that child? I thought so. All the circumstances pointed to that conclusion. Yet it didn't happen. Did I misread God's will? I don't think so. So how do we understand what happened?

The Bible teaches us a great deal about God's purposes and will for his people. One of God's main purposes is to make us more like him. Psalm 23:3 says, "He guides me in paths of righteousness for his name's sake." Paths of righteousness have to do with character development—shaping our inner self. In the process of spiritual maturity, there are certain things that God desires us to be, or become (see Diagram 2.2). Although this is not a comprehensive list, some of the things God wants us to *be* as we mature include:

- Patient (Romans 12:12; Galatians 5:22; Ephesians 4:2; 1 Thessalonians 5:14; James 5:7-8,10)
- Joyful (Psalm 66:1; Psalm 97:11; Proverbs 23:24; Acts 2:28; Romans 12:12; 1 Thessalonians 5:16)

- Hopeful (Acts 2:26; Romans 5:4-5; Romans 8:25; Romans 15:4; Hebrews 6:19; 1 Peter 1:13)
- Humble (2 Chronicles 7:14; Matthew 23:12; Romans 12:16; Ephesians 4:2; 1 Peter 5:6)
- Forgiving (Matthew 6:12,14; Matthew 18:21-22; Ephesians 4:32; Colossians 3:13)
- Merciful (Matthew 5:7; Matthew 12:7; Luke 6:36; James 3:17; Jude 22)
- Kind (Proverbs 11:17; Proverbs 14:21; 1 Corinthians 13:4; Ephesians 4:32; Colossians 3:12; 1 Thessalonians 5:15)
- Filled with the Spirit (Acts 2:4; Acts 4:31; Acts 9:17; Ephesians 5:18)
- Obedient (Deuteronomy 6:3; Psalm 119:17,34; John 14:15,23-24; 1 John 5:3; 2 John 6)
- Faithful (Proverbs 2:8; Matthew 25:23; Romans 12:12; Galatians 5:22; Revelation 2:10; Revelation 14:12)
- Trusting (Proverbs 3:5; Proverbs 22:19; Isaiah 26:4; John 14:1; Romans 15:13; Hebrews 2:13)
- Loving (Proverbs 3:3; Mark 12:31,33; John 13:34; John 15:9,17; Romans 13:10; Ephesians 5:1-2)
- Holy (Romans 12:1; 1 Corinthians 1:2; Ephesians 1:4; 1 Thessalonians 4:7; 2 Timothy 1:9; 1 Peter 1:15-16)
- Self-controlled (Galatians 5:23; 1 Thessalonians 5:6,8; 1 Peter 1:13; 1 Peter 4:7; 1 Peter 5:8)
- Pure (Matthew 5:8; Philippians 1:10; 1 Timothy 4:12; 1 Timothy 5:22; Titus 2:5; 1 John 3:3)
- Gentle (Proverbs 15:1; Galatians 5:23; Ephesians 4:2; Philippians 4:5; Colossians 3:12; 1 Timothy 6:11)
- Imitators of God (Ephesians 5:1; 1 Thessalonians 1:6)

- Like Jesus (Romans 8:29; 1 Corinthians 15:49; 2 Corinthians 3:18; Ephesians 4:24)

Diagram 2.2

In addition to leading us in paths of righteousness by shaping our character, God also leads us in the paths of life (Psalm 16:11). As we try to discern God's will, we should remember that he has already revealed much of what we are to *do* in order to live our lives in a way that pleases him—in a way that matters for all eternity (see Diagram 2.3). For example:

- Love him with all of our heart (Deuteronomy 30:16,20; Matthew 22:37; Mark 12:30; Luke 10:27)
- Obey him (Joshua 22:5; John 14:15; Romans 16:26; 2 Corinthians 2:9; Hebrews 5:8-9; 1 Peter 1:14; 2 John 6)
- Trust him (Psalm 9:10; Psalm 13:5; Psalm 56:3-4,11; Proverbs 3:5; Isaiah 8:17; Isaiah 26:3-4; John 12:36; John 14:1)
- Pray (Psalm 32:6; Matthew 6:9; Mark 14:38; Ephesians 6:18; Colossians 4:2; 1 Thessalonians 5:17; James 5:13)
- Believe (Mark 5:36; John 20:31; Acts 16:31; Romans 10:10; Galatians 3:22; Ephesians 1:18-19)
- Make every effort to keep unity (Romans 15:5; Ephesians 4:2; Hebrews 12:14; 1 Peter 3:11)
- Submit to one another (Ephesians 5:21; James 3:17)

- Respect those in authority (Romans 13:1; 1 Thessalonians 5:12; Titus 3:1; Hebrews 13:17)
- Glorify God by our life (Psalm 63:3; Romans 15:6; 1 Corinthians 10:31; 2 Corinthians 3:18; Revelation 14:7)
- Love one another (John 13:34; John 15:12; Romans 12:10; Romans 13:10; Galatians 5:14; 1 Thessalonians 4:9-10)
- Devote ourselves to doing good (Romans 12:9; 2 Corinthians 9:8; Galatians 6:9-10; Titus 3:1,8,14)
- Give to those who are in need (Proverbs 14:21; Matthew 6:2-3; Romans 12:13; 1 John 3:16-18)
- Forgive those who sin against us (Matthew 6:12,14; Matthew 18:21-22; Ephesians 4:32; Colossians 3:13)
- Witness to others (Matthew 5:16; Matthew 28:19; Mark 16:15; Acts 1:8)
- Overcome evil with good (Proverbs 25:21; Romans 12:21; 1 Thessalonians 5:15; 1 Peter 2:15-22; 1 Peter 3:9,17)
- Love our enemies (Matthew 5:44,46; Luke 6:27,32,35; Romans 12:20)
- Give thanks (1 Chronicles 16:8; Psalm 30:12; Psalm 107:1; Ephesians 5:20; 1 Thessalonians 5:18)

Diagram 2.3

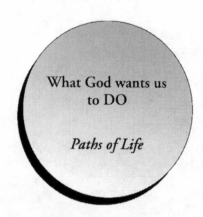

What God wants us to DO

Paths of Life

Also, God's Word says he will teach us to walk in the paths of wisdom and truth (Psalm 32:8; Psalm 25:4; Proverbs 4:11). This third circle (see Diagram 2.4) represents our personal choices, made within the boundaries of wisdom, prayer, and God's Word. This is the area we Christians tend to give the most attention to when trying to understand God's will in a particular dilemma or circumstance. I believe Scripture teaches us that God gives us the freedom to choose, for example, whom we will marry, what job we will take, what city to live in, and myriad other things—as long as they don't violate the principles for godly living outlined in his Word. When seeking God's will, we often look for confirmation, evidenced by good results, that we made the right choice. Then we feel reassured that our choice was indeed God's will. However, if it seems that our decision leads to poor or unexpected results, we often question whether we acted on God's will or whether we "missed it."

After much prayer and guidance from other Christians, Sam

Diagram 2.4

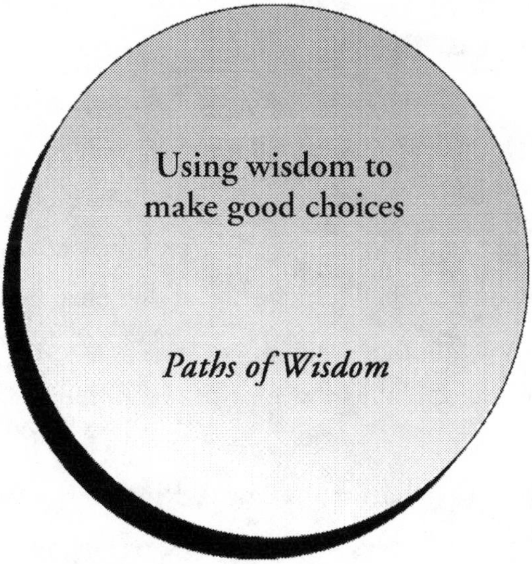

Using wisdom to make good choices

Paths of Wisdom

decided to move his family all the way to California because of a terrific job opportunity. After three months, his new company folded. He now questions whether his decision was in line with God's will. Again, human perspective tends to seek positive results to confirm God's will.

But God's perspective is different from ours. God uses the difficult circumstances in which we find ourselves to bring about his will in our lives—to help us become more like Jesus. Sam and his family will face hardship and trouble as a result of their move and subsequent job loss. However, during and because of this trouble Sam and his family will be stretched to pray more, to forgive those who may have not been truthful with them, to trust God more, to believe God more, and to be more merciful than they have ever been before. This is one way in which God uses trouble to nurture Christlike character in our lives. Sam's decision to move to California may have been God's will, not for any temporal satisfaction, but for the maturity and growth of Sam and his family. God is more concerned with the two inner circles—what he wants us to *be* and *do*—and often uses our personal choices to lead us toward greater maturity (see Diagram 2.5). We, on the other hand, tend to be more concerned with the outer circle—the result of our choices—because we tend to weigh our temporal happiness more heavily than we weigh God's eternal purposes.

Recently a woman contemplating divorce came to see me. She was a Christian and struggled with guilt. "I'm definitely not happy, and feel I made the wrong choice," she cried. "I didn't obey God and should never have married him. It wasn't God's will, so now do I have to live the rest of my life with a man who isn't right for me?"

This woman is hurting. What do we say to her? If we think that it's God's will for us to be happy, we will advise this woman to leave her husband and pursue a new, more satisfying relationship. If we believe only in adhering to rules, we will tell her the Bible forbids divorce except in cases of adultery; therefore, she has to stay married. But if we see what God is up to in her life by gaining an eternal perspective, we can encourage her that this season is an opportunity for her to deepen her faith, to learn to trust God with her life in new ways. This time of trouble will give her a chance to live her life in more meaningful ways than living in pursuit of personal happiness. And maybe, in the midst of her transformation, God will bring changes about in her marriage.

Ultimately, God's will for Christians is to bring us into an intimate relationship with him and conform us to the image of Christ. Contrary to prosperity theology, God's will is not to give us a happy and carefree life. In our troubles he promises, "And we know that in all things God works for the good of those who love him, who have been called according to his purpose. For those God foreknew he also predestined

Diagram 2.5

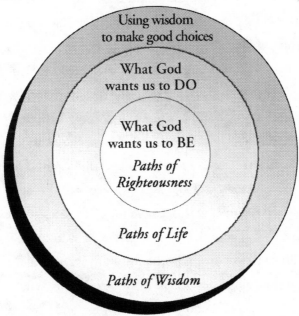

Using wisdom
to make good choices

What God
wants us to DO

What God
wants us to BE

*Paths of
Righteousness*

Paths of Life

Paths of Wisdom

to be conformed to the likeness of his Son, that he might be the first-born among many brothers" (Romans 8:28-29). These verses are familiar to most Christians, but do you value them? Have you tucked them in your heart as an anchor for your soul when waves of troubles threaten to overtake you?

In addition to understanding what God is up to in shaping our character, it is also helpful to understand how God uses life's troubles to deepen our relationship with him. As I struggled with the adoption that never was, I was forced to take a hard look at who I thought God was. One of the ways God did this for me was by challenging the split between the knowledge in my head and the beliefs in my heart.

For example, 1 John 1:5 says, "God is light; in him there is no darkness at all." What did that mean to me in light of my struggle? At the moment, it meant nothing. They were words on a page, something I knew in my head but that held no value in my heart. If they had, I might have responded differently to the pain and sadness I was feeling. During my struggle, God sought to teach me who he truly is by exposing my false picture of him. If God is a God who does not lie, then the fact that he is holy and has no darkness in his character at all ought to comfort me in the midst of my pain. But this truth can comfort me only if I *believe* him.

Instead of viewing the character of God through the lens of my circumstances or troubles, I began to push circumstances aside to see God for who he said he is (see Diagram 2.6). The Holy Spirit challenged my heart to revise my view of God. Whose voice was I going to listen to about who God is and how he acts: the voice of my hurt feelings or the voice of God? Was I going to value what he said? Was I going to believe him? I could no longer keep Christianity in my intellect alone; that was not enough. I would either believe it with my whole heart, or I would walk away. Although I do not understand why God allowed the birth mother to deceive us, I have come to know—because there is no darkness in his character—that God does not deceive, trick, or maliciously treat his children. And in that I can take comfort.

How God Uses Trials and Troubles

To Get Our Attention—To Reorient Us to What Is True and Important

Many of us keep our eyes on the temporal plane, satisfied with living our lives for the main goal of personal happiness. Others of us live our lives in such a rush of activity that we leave no time to be reflective. As a consequence, our relationship with God is put on the back burner. Although God is not opposed to personal happiness or even meaningful activities,

Diagram 2.6

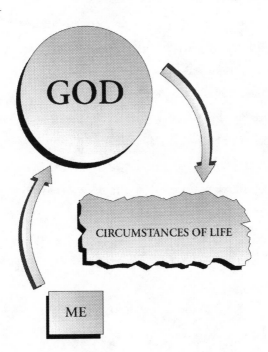

he defines them differently than we do and at times disrupts our personal happiness and our activities in order to bring us into a deeper encounter with him.

In Deuteronomy 6:10-12 Moses warned the people, "When the LORD your God brings you into the land he swore to your fathers, to Abraham, Isaac and Jacob, to give you—a land with large, flourishing cities you did not build, houses filled with all kinds of good things you did not provide, wells you did not dig, and vineyards and olive groves you did not plant—then when you eat and are satisfied, be careful that you do not forget the LORD, who brought you out of Egypt, out of the land of slavery."

Fénelon, a seventeenth-century Christian mystic, said, "It is in his tender and fatherly breast that we forget him. It is because of the sweetness of his gifts that we stop thinking of him. What he gives us every moment, instead of touching us, diverts us."[3]

Doesn't God often get our undivided attention when adversity hits? Other things immediately lose their lure, and we focus on him instead of everything else.

David called me in a frenzy. He had just discovered his wife of fifteen years with another man. Distraught, he didn't know where to turn or what to do. All of a sudden, his baseball game and motorcycle racing didn't seem nearly so important as they had been. Now prayer, seeking God, and trying to win his wife back were priorities in his life; yesterday, they had been secondary.

TO DETACH OUR HEART FROM TEMPORAL PLEASURES OR TEMPORAL REALITIES

We are easily deceived and lulled into a love affair with the world. Temporal delights bind our hearts to the pleasures of the world and act as an anesthetic to deaden the deeper longings of our heart. Sometimes God in his wisdom allows troubles to come our way to snatch us away from the cords of death—death of our soul. Esau sold his birthright for a pot of porridge. Our birthright as Christians is to become like Christ. But many of us sell it for the temporal pleasures of the world. Even legitimate pleasures can tempt us to linger at the table of cheap substitutes instead of hungering after the bread of life. God in his sovereign love may need to interrupt this pattern in order to detach our heart from our temporal loves and bring us into a deeper relationship with him.

TO DEEPEN OUR ROOTS—ATTACHING OUR HEARTS TO THE GOOD AND THE TRUE

A plant deprived of nutrients will die, but a plant that gets too much of a good thing will also become weak. All my gardening books caution against overwatering plants, which causes them to develop shallow roots and become more vulnerable to decay and disease. Experts suggest allowing the surface soil to dry out in order to force the roots to forge deeper for the water it needs.

When I was in college, my father built a log cabin in the Upper Peninsula of Michigan. On occasion my family has had the opportunity to vacation there. One day he suggested that he, my five-year-old daughter, Amanda (yes, we did eventually adopt another child), and I go exploring and take a walk around the lake. It would be good exercise—about three miles around. Walking easily along the dirt path, Amanda skipped about fifty yards ahead, confident that we were close behind. My father and I walked together in quiet solitude. About halfway around, we took a path that stayed closer to the water, but the terrain changed. It became hilly and was full of fallen branches, tree stumps, and rocks. We had to watch our every step. Amanda quickly drew back and grabbed my hand. During one particularly difficult climb my father reached down and grabbed my hand. He held it throughout the rest of the walk. Never before in my whole life had my father held my hand. I almost cried. The difficult terrain we walked together gave me an opportunity to experience my father in a new way—one that deeply touched my heart. I will never forget it.

During the difficult times of life God never leaves our side. Sometimes we don't experience his presence, but that doesn't mean he is not present. Waiting out the moment instead of trying to rush the process forward toward resolution or relief yields deeper roots of love and trust.

TO SHAPE HIS NATURE IN US

In Hebrews 5:8 we learn that Jesus learned obedience through the things he suffered. I've often wondered: If Jesus was perfect, why did he need to learn obedience? Perhaps obedience doesn't come naturally. Although Jesus was sinless, his flesh had to come under the authority and control of God the Father.

Romans 5:3-4 tells us that "suffering produces perseverance; perseverance, character; and character, hope." Knowing what God is up to is one part of the journey. But as Henry Blackaby notes in his book *Experiencing God*, it is then up to us whether we will join him in cooperating with his plan for us—or fight against him.[4] Is there suffering in obedience? Sure. Is there pain in life's troubles? Sometimes excruciating pain. But joy comes when we can rest in the knowledge that God is shaping our hearts—cutting away all the fat, all the things that are contrary to his image in us.

> Make me fruitful by living to that love,
> my character becoming more beautiful every day.

If traces of Christ's love-artistry be upon me,
>   may he work on with his divine brush
>   until the complete image be obtained
>   and I be made a perfect copy of him, my master.[5]

TO REFLECT HIS GLORY

The Westminster Catechism states that the chief end of man is to glorify God and enjoy him forever.[6] Many of us live as though our chief end is to be happy and fulfilled. We live for self and not for God. Often God allows the troubles in our life to give us a chance to live for a higher purpose than our own satisfaction.

Many years ago I read a novel about a family who lived through World War II and experienced the horror of the German concentration camps. One particular scene grabbed my attention, and I have reflected on it numerous times throughout the years. Two men are in a horrific Nazi prison camp. They see the tremendous cruelty and evil that man's heart is capable of. They see those they love die. They are hungry and sick, yet they choose to be rays of light in a very dark place. At one point one says to the other:

> "No. It is not fear of hell that turns my heart from evil." Theo smiled to himself as though he had discovered a secret. "We have been privileged to see what becomes of men who give themselves over to darkness. They are no longer men. They are the creatures; we are still men." He reached out to touch the arm of the professor. "And yet, we all began exactly alike, like lumps of coal, maybe in different shapes and sizes. The fire and the pressure of hatred consumes some men until they consume others around them in a white-hot fire. And others, trapped in

the same fierce pressure and terrible heat, become diamonds to glisten in the hand of God. To shine bright when the blackness is all around, to find love when others are burning in their hatred. Isn't that the essence of God?"[7]

God often allows troubles to give us the opportunity to reflect his glory in the midst of our pain. Not too long ago a particular passage of Scripture caught my attention, and I began meditating on it. It was one of those quick prayers by Jesus, but it had a profound effect on me. Jesus prayed, "Now my heart is troubled, and what shall I say? 'Father, save me from this hour'? No, it was for this very reason I came to this hour. Father, glorify your name!" (John 12:27).

In the past, how often I had prayed, "Save me from this trouble!" instead of asking God to use the situation to bring him glory. Recently, during some midlife health problems, I had the opportunity to pray differently. I told God that whatever happened, what I wanted most was for him to be glorified in the process. I believe that had I not been meditating on that verse in John for months before my health troubles hit, I would not have prayed that way. What a miraculous change God had brought about in my heart! It wasn't that I didn't want to be healed; I did. But I wanted something else *more*. I wanted God to be glorified in my life, in whatever way he chose. This time in my prayer, I was becoming like Jesus. What joy in the midst of my trouble!

WHAT DOES MY HEART WANT IN LIFE?

If we are honest, we will admit we don't ever want to be propelled into darkness. We don't want to have troubles hit us from behind. Most of

us want happiness in life and relief from difficult circumstances. The spiritual person wants those things too, but he is willing to forsake them for something far more important and wonderful—the opportunity to know and glorify God. Sometimes God asks us to sacrifice our temporal happiness in order to give glory to him.

Lest you think I have mastered the troubles of life, I recently grumbled and complained when my brand-new treadmill broke. Sometimes the little irritants of life, more than anything else, rob me of the opportunity to be like Jesus. We recognize the big stuff as sacred moments and rise to the occasion. But the everyday troubles and trials of life—the child spilling her milk, the washing machine overflowing, the car breaking down, the teenager smarting off—all stir something deep inside of us that craves and demands something that only God has: control! We want control over our world and can't stand it when life rips it out of our hands.

Submitting ourselves to God's will requires a change of heart. It takes trust—trust in a God who is too pure and too holy to allow any evil in our lives unless it can be used for the exceedingly good purpose of making us more like Christ. In his book *Trusting God*, Jerry Bridges quotes, "God in His love always wills what is best for us. In His wisdom He always knows what is best, and in His sovereignty He has the power to bring it about."[8]

SEEING REALITY WITH A
HEAVENLY PERSPECTIVE

Several years ago my family took a trip to Walt Disney World and visited MGM Studios. One ride, Star Wars Adventure, was especially

thrilling. About fifteen people sat in a simulated space capsule, seat belts fastened. R2D2 was our guide, and we were going to take a pretend ride through space. All of a sudden an accident propelled our capsule to a distant galaxy. Traveling the speed of light, our little spaceship barely maneuvered itself through caves and around stars, meteors, and unidentifiable objects. The ride was quite realistic, and but for the fact that everyone knew it was just a ride, we would have been terrified. After we safely landed, I thought to myself, *Perhaps this is what life would be like if we could always have God's perspective.* We would not be so terrified when trials and troubles come, because we would know that what we were going through was not all there is to "true reality." When James tells us to consider it all joy when we have trials and troubles, his advice doesn't seem possible to our finite minds. But just as it is craziness to laugh at being hurled into darkest space, it seems like craziness to be joyful in our most sorrowful times. Yet the perspective that kept me from panic on the ride—knowing that it was just a ride—is the same kind of perspective that keeps me from despair in times of great pain and trouble—knowing that this life is not all there is, and that true reality is much bigger than I can see right now.

The apostle Paul experienced difficult troubles. In 2 Corinthians he tells us, "We are hard pressed on every side, but not crushed; perplexed, but not in despair; persecuted, but not abandoned; struck down, but not destroyed." I've often wondered how Paul kept this perspective. I've felt crushed, despairing, abandoned, and destroyed, but Paul didn't. What was his secret? Later on in the same chapter he tells us: "Therefore we do not lose heart. Though outwardly we are wasting away, yet inwardly we are being renewed day by day. For our light and momentary troubles are achieving for us an eternal glory

that far outweighs them all. So we fix our eyes not on what is seen but on what is unseen. For what is seen is temporary, but what is unseen is eternal."

"This world is not our home" is a familiar saying to most Christians. Nevertheless, our heart remains attached to many good (and sometimes not-so-good) things in this world. God, out of his great love for us, draws our heart toward him, asking us to completely abandon ourselves to faith and trust. Having heavenly perspective gives us strength to endure the process of suffering while still living in this world. Perspective helps a woman endure the pain of childbirth for the joy of having a child. Perspective helps the sick choose difficult and painful surgery in order to improve their quality of life. Hebrews 12 tells us that perspective—or looking toward a higher purpose or goal—helped Jesus endure the cross.

At times God brings light into our soul to shine truth and give us that perspective. Other times it seems he sits by and allows deep darkness to roll in like a thick black smoke that threatens to choke off our spiritual life. It is in this dark place that most of us look for the nearest exit. We don't want to stay still and will do just about anything we can to find relief.

But if we can learn to wait, we will find that something miraculous happens while we are most helpless. Remember my despair over the failed adoption? God never brought light to that situation. I will never know why the birth mother chose another family. But much like a seed needs the dark deep earth to sprout roots, for me, the deep soil of despair and darkness cultivated a new walk with God. It is there that I began my journey toward really knowing God for who he says he is, not for what I thought he should be.

My parakeet, Sydney, and I have limited perspective. We only see a small part of true reality. God desires for us to trust him when we can't see. He seeks to change our heart to his perspective so we can see more clearly. Are you willing?

> LORD, HIGH AND HOLY, MEEK AND LOWLY,
> Thou has brought me to the valley of vision,
>> where I live in the depths but see thee in the heights;
>> hemmed in by mountains of sin I behold thy glory.
> Let me learn by paradox
>> that the way down is the way up,
>> that to be low is to be high,
>> that the broken heart is the healed heart,
>> that the contrite spirit is the rejoicing spirit,
>> that the repenting soul is the victorious soul,
>> that to have nothing is to possess all,
>> that to bear the cross is to wear the crown,
>> that to give is to receive,
>> that the valley is the place of vision.
> Lord, in the daytime stars can be seen from deepest wells,
>> and the deeper the wells the brighter thy stars shine;
> Let me find thy light in my darkness,
>> thy life in my death,
>> thy joy in my sorrow,
>> thy grace in my sin,
>> thy riches in my poverty,
>> thy glory in my valley.
>
> —"The Valley of Vision"[9]

Time for Reflection

1. Are you in agreement with God that what he is up to in your life is good and for your good? If not, what would it take for him to convince you? Ask him boldly for this thing, as we know that this is his will for you. What inner struggles do you have in abandoning your heart to God's design for your life?

2. Does your heart long for the good life or the spiritual life? One means living for self and the other means total abandonment to God. Reflect and meditate on Oswald Chambers's statement:

Faith is not pathetic sentiment, but robust vigorous confidence built on the fact that God is holy love. You cannot see Him just now, you cannot understand what He is doing, but you know *Him*. Shipwreck occurs where there is not that mental poise which comes from being established on the eternal truth that God is holy love. Faith is the heroic effort of your life, you fling yourself in reckless confidence on God.[10]

3. Begin to pray as Jesus did in the midst of your life's troubles. Use John 12:27-28 as your guide.

Dear Lord,
I am beginning to get a picture of what you are doing in my life
through my troubles. Instead of always asking you for relief or

help to get out of my troubles, help me to be willing to be made like Jesus. Help my heart to be willing to be used by you for your glory and your purposes during my troubles. Lord, in order to fully trust you I need to know you better. I need to know your heart as always good and always for my good. I desire to trust you even when I don't understand you. Increase my faith that I might see more of your eternal perspective and less of the temporal pleasures that would steal me away. Change my heart, Lord. Make my heart like Jesus' heart. Amen

CHAPTER THREE

OUR RESPONSE TO LIFE'S TROUBLES

Give careful thought to your ways.

HAGGAI 1:7

Jack and Mary came to counseling over troubles in their marriage.

"If only Mary would realize how angry I get when she doesn't put the pens back in the drawer!" he shouted. "I can't stand it anymore. She's driving me crazy with her lack of organization and just plain stupidity."

Mary wept as Jack continued his barrage of complaints against her.

Next it was Mary's turn. "I know I upset Jack. I'm not a great housekeeper. I lose things easily. But"—and she looked pleadingly at Jack—"I can't take it anymore either. I feel like I can never do anything right. You're always angry with me."

When troubles come our way, most of us respond by trying to change the situation or the person we believe causes the trouble in our life. Jack wanted Mary to change by becoming more organized and careful. Mary wanted Jack to change by becoming less angry and more accepting.

Our biggest button pushers in life are usually the people we interact with and are closest to. We find ourselves wishing they would change so that we would be happier—or at least not so angry or frustrated. We tell ourselves that if only they would be more loving, more submissive, more dominant, more obedient, more respectful, more helpful, more whatever, then we could respond better to them and not get so upset. We play a waiting game: I'll change if or when you do.

To get out of this no-win pattern, however, we must begin to see that it is our relationship with God, not another person's actions or lack of actions, that will help us to grow, change, and respond rightly. In order to mature, we need to understand that our responses to life's troubles don't come from outside of us (our situation); they come from inside of us (our heart). The *NIV Study Bible* defines *heart* as "the center of the human spirit, from which spring emotions, thought, motivations, courage and action."[1] As we begin to "give careful thought to our ways"—specifically, the way we feel, the way we think, and the way we act—we can begin to understand ourselves better.

THE IMPORTANCE OF SELF-EXAMINATION

Plato said a life unexamined is not worth living.[2] Examining ourselves is not an easy process and is often set into motion by the troubles or tests that we face. The word *examine* means to study or scrutinize something. In many industries certain materials are closely examined or tested in order to measure the integrity of the object. For example, in the aerospace industry, regular and rigorous testing takes place on many airplane components to make sure the parts meet certain requirements for reliability and safety. This testing is necessary to prevent the use of defective components, which may cause a catastrophic failure while the plane is flying. The tests help inspectors discover weaknesses and identify possible design malfunctions so that the manufacturers can fix the flaws and ultimately create a better component.

When I was in school, math was never my strong suit, especially those tricky word problems. No matter how much I thought I understood specific concepts, working them out in the practical applications presented by word problems was a different story. Those word problems revealed what I didn't know or couldn't apply.

Ideally, school examinations measure the integrity of what students have learned and reveal areas where they haven't grasped the concepts. Those examinations benefit not only the professors (by providing a standard for grades), but they also benefit the students (by revealing what the student actually knows). The test is the proof.

As Christians, many of us know a great deal about the things of God. We have read the Bible and many other good books about living the Christian life. Yet when we try to put those biblical concepts into practice, we stumble. Like my trouble with word problems, we find that what we know on one level we can't necessarily apply on another.

James 1:12 says that when we have passed the test God gives us, we will receive the crown of life. What is the test? Often the troubles in our lives test the reality or the integrity of our faith. How do we respond to the troubles God allows to come our way? The test isn't for God's benefit; he already knows what is in our heart. The test is for our benefit; it reveals to us the weaknesses in our faith and trust in God.

My rage toward God when the adoption fell through revealed a shallowness in my knowledge of him. As I gave vent to my rage, I said things like "You are not good," "You are not trustworthy," "You are not who you say you are," "How can I possibly trust a God who tricks his people to trust him and then lets them down?"

In some cases, anger may be an appropriate response to the situation—for example, my anger with the birth mother for lying to us and betraying our trust. But my rage was against God and who he claimed to be. I didn't know him as he described himself, and this became apparent in the midst of my trouble. When I didn't get what I wanted or expected, my faith fell apart. God showed me that my relationship with him wasn't as strong as I had thought it was. He knew my love was academic and shallow. It was because of his love for me that he wanted me to know it. Why? So I wouldn't deceive myself.

God tests us because of his great love for us. He knows our tendency to deceive ourselves and to be deceived by outside influences. Our relationship with God is so important that he doesn't want us to fool ourselves, thinking that by merely following the rules of our particular denomination or by subscribing to certain creeds we have relationship with him while our hearts may be a long way from loving him. In Matthew 7, Jesus describes a group of people who thought they knew God but actually never did. Paul tells us to examine ourselves to see if we are in the faith (2 Corinthians 13:5). The apostle John warns us against self-deception (1 John 1:8).

Examining our responses to troubles is an opportunity to see whether we are applying the things we think we believe to the real-life troubles that come our way. We will see the weak areas and the things in us that God wants to change. As we come to understand our own responses, we need to remind ourselves of what God is up to—he's walking us through the process of maturing us and developing the nature of Christ within us. Keeping this goal in mind, we can press on through our troubles, trusting God and deepening our roots of love and faith in him who loves us.

Understanding Our Responses to Troubles

My husband coaches a girls' volleyball team. Sometimes when he teaches a skill he will videotape a player and then show her the tape in slow motion so that the two of them can examine each component of her movements and make necessary changes. We don't typically think of our responses to trouble as something that can be broken down and separated. But as part of our self-examination, we will need to identify the various components of our responses in order to understand them more fully and see where we can make changes. We must do this to stop playing the I'll-change-when-you-change game.

As we examine our responses to the troubles we experience, we will begin to understand that our responses come from what is going on inside us, not from another person's behavior. Actions arise out of our heart as we respond with *our* feelings, *our* thoughts, and *our* behaviors.

THE WAY WE FEEL

Every trouble we face calls forth an emotional response from us. How do you *feel* when you are in the midst of trouble? Do you feel irritated? Discouraged? Angry? Pressured? Guilty? Anxious? Most of us, if we are honest, don't experience the more positive emotions in the midst of our troubles. We don't feel happy, content, joyful, peaceful, or relaxed. We feel upset! If we were to diagram the way we feel in response to our troubles, it might look like Chart 3.1 on page 62.

The next time one of life's troubles comes your way, whether large or small, try to pay attention to the emotions you are feeling in the midst of it. You may begin to see a pattern in your emotional response to troubles. For example, when Jack began to take notice of his emotions, he realized that they frequently fell into the family of angry feelings, such as irritated, impatient, ticked off, frustrated, furious, or enraged. On the other hand, Mary noticed that her feelings fell more into the family of anxious responses. She most often felt fearful, worried, uncertain, nervous, panicky, or scared in the midst of her troubles.

Some people find it difficult to identify what they feel and often say, "I don't know, I just feel upset." If that happens to you, the next time you are upset try to sort out your feelings by asking yourself, Am I feeling sad? If not sad, then am I mad? What about scared? Or perhaps you have a feeling of hurt. Once you can discern the general category of feeling, try to narrow it further; go up or down the scale of intensity. Are you very sad? Are you a little bit scared? Different words describe various intensities of emotions. For example, a little bit angry is *irritated.* A great deal of anger is *furious. Terrified* describes a heart full of fear, and a little *nervous* is a less intense version of *anxious.*

Other people find it difficult to identify or admit their feelings because they believe or have been taught that as Christians they "should" or "shouldn't" feel certain emotions. They struggle to be honest with themselves and admit what they really do feel if it's not what they or others expect them to feel.

Debra came to counseling troubled over her relationship with her

Chart 3.1

Troubles	Common Feeling Response
sitting in a traffic jam	irritation, impatience, frustration, anxiousness
getting laid off from a job	pain, sadness, anger, fear
losing a loved one	grief, rage, confusion, depression

mother. She described her mother as dependent and fearful. "I just don't know how to help her," Debra said. As I probed further, she told me of a time when her mother sat sobbing as Debra told her she couldn't stay for dinner. I asked Debra how she felt when her mother cried. She hesitated. Then after a long pause she said, "I feel so guilty. I shouldn't feel upset with her. I hate myself for having awful thoughts about my mother. I should love her." Debra was stuck. She could not admit she felt angry and frustrated with her mother's dependency and manipulative behavior. She felt too guilty and ashamed to admit it to me or even to herself and was instead flooded with self-hatred.

It is important to be honest with yourself and name your feelings, even when you wish you weren't feeling a particular emotion. When I felt furious with God over the failed adoption, it did me no good to deny it to myself. Only when I faced my anger was I able to eventually see it for what it was and work through it.

Our emotions are a very real part of who we are as human beings. Examining ourselves means becoming aware of what we feel. Jesus experienced a full range of human emotions. At times he felt angry, disappointed, and sad. As he faced the horror of the Cross he felt apprehensive, and as he hung dying he felt abandoned. Becoming more like Christ doesn't mean cutting ourselves off from our feelings or pretending that we only feel the more positive range of emotions.

It is crucial to be honest with ourselves about how we feel; however, it is not always helpful to share every feeling we have with someone else. Our emotions can be intense and real, but—unlike Jesus' emotions—they are also tainted with our own sin and pride. In our psychologized culture we have become emotional exhibitionists and are encouraged to "let it all out" for the sake of feeling better. But God never endorses such self-centered motives. If my children are annoying me at the moment, I need to recognize and admit how I am feeling. It may or may not be wise to share those feelings with my children. Perhaps I'm just being selfish and my children need my attention even though I would rather not be bothered. It may be more helpful for me to withdraw for a moment of prayer and share with God how I feel. Being aware and honest with myself is not the same as letting it all hang out. Some things are better left tucked in. Our feelings ought to inform us, not control us.

Identifying our feelings and understanding where they are coming from helps us better decide what to do with them. At times, it can be beneficial to express our feelings to the people involved. At other times, expressing feelings is like dropping a lit match on gasoline and can cause incredible damage. Although the old nursery rhyme told us that words will never hurt us, it is simply not true. We have done too much damage to people we love by blurting out ugly feelings at the moment of their greatest intensity. Blurting might provide some sort of cathartic relief, but it is never beneficial to the hearer or to the relationship. I liken blurting to vomiting: We feel better getting it out, but vomit belongs in the toilet, not on another person. A healthier way to get destructive or negative feelings out is to journal them. We can find a release from the intensity of our emotions when we write them down or offer them up to God in prayer. In that process, we may also get some perspective and guidance on what to do with them.

Often our feelings act as a warning light that something is amiss in ourselves or in our relationships. Ignoring them can lead to greater problems. Identifying and admitting what we feel is a crucial part of self-examination.

The next response to examine is our thoughts. When I was raging at God, my emotions were intense. I felt hurt, betrayed, angry, and sad.

My thoughts revealed my mistrust of God and how I viewed God's hand in the situation. By listening to our thoughts we can start to understand our problem and work toward a change of heart.

THE WAY WE THINK

We are thinking creatures. We are continuously having an internal dialogue in order to make sense of the world around us.

If you are a parent or if you interact with small children, you have probably chuckled over the way they interpret life around them. When my husband had to take a business trip to San Francisco, Ryan, then three, asked me, "Mom, who is Sam?"

"Sam who?" I responded.

"You know, Sam from Cisco," he said.

Ryan knew his dad went to San Francisco, but he had no established category in his brain that could accurately process what San Francisco was. The only way he could make meaning of the information was to process it into the categories he already knew. He knew Sam was the name of a person. That was enough. He concluded his dad went to visit a man named Sam—from Cisco.

Our thoughts act as a filter or lens through which we view and make sense of our circumstances. In this process we participate in an internal dialogue, by which we constantly interpret what is happening around us. Our *thoughts* about any given situation, not the situation itself, determine to a significant extent our emotional reaction to it.

Cognitive therapy is a secular therapy that developed in the fifties out of a growing dissatisfaction with the psychoanalytic model for treating people with emotional problems. Through clinical studies researchers observed that depressed people, for example, regularly saw the world in negative ways. In other words, their way of thinking became a lens through which they evaluated all their experiences. From there, the cognitive therapists discovered that our thinking about a situation shapes our emotional responses to that situation.

Consider this example: Late one night you are home alone watching television. Your family is out for the evening, and you aren't expecting them in for quite some time. Suddenly the back doorknob starts rattling. What emotion do you feel? If you are wired like the average person, you feel scared—either a little or a lot, but scared would be the general category of emotion. Why? Because the doorknob is rattling? No. You feel scared because you interpreted the rattling of the doorknob to mean something. What are your thoughts about the doorknob rattling? You think that someone is trying to break into your house. That thought is a perfectly logical interpretation about the situation, and your body and emotions respond appropriately with feelings of fear. As your body pumps adrenaline and your mind races with battle plans, the door flings open and your college-age son steps into the kitchen with a big grin and says, "Hi, I'm home. I got out early."

Now what do you feel? Probably relief mixed with a bit of anger at your son for scaring you. Why have your emotions so suddenly changed from panic to relief? Because now you are no longer *thinking* that an intruder is breaking into your house. You realize that your initial interpretation of the situation was understandable but false. Your thoughts now have changed and your emotions follow suit.

Cognitive therapists thought they had discovered something new, but God's Word teaches that our thoughts are crucial to our well-being. Proverbs 23:7 says "as he thinketh in his heart, so is he" (KJV). The key to better understanding our emotions is to realize that they are not based on what is happening to us but on what we *think* is happening to us. As long as we believe that an intruder is at our door, our emotions of fear and panic are going to be quite real. Our emotional response to our troubles is based on how we think about them or how we interpret them—accurately or inaccurately, true or not.

Bonnie came to counseling because she had poor self-esteem. She described herself as feeling depressed and lonely. She said she was a loser and that no one liked her. One particular day she was hurt by a friend who ignored her at a church service. Bonnie's trouble in the moment was her friend's ignoring her. Bonnie felt hurt and lonely. When I asked her what kinds of thoughts she had about the incident, she said, "She doesn't really want to be my friend" and "She is probably mad at me for something I did." When I asked her what evidence she had to support such thoughts, Bonnie shrugged and said she didn't really have any except that her friend hadn't said hi on Sunday.

"Perhaps there's another way of looking at your friend's actions, Bonnie," I coached. "What other reasons might she have had not to say hi to you this past week?"

"I can't imagine," Bonnie said. "Well—maybe she just didn't see me. Maybe she was preoccupied."

I encouraged Bonnie to give her friend the benefit of the doubt and not to jump to conclusions. To Bonnie's surprise, the following Sunday Bonnie's friend gave her a big smile and said, "Hi! I missed you last week. Weren't you here?" Bonnie was shocked. It was true that her friend hadn't seen her. She wasn't purposely ignoring her.

Bonnie suffered genuine and intense feelings of hurt and sadness the previous week—not because her friend didn't say hi, but because Bonnie interpreted her friend's behaviors in a negative way. When Bonnie changed her thoughts about the situation, her emotions were not as painful. When we start examining our thoughts as well as identifying our feelings, we recognize that some of the thoughts we have about our trouble are untrue.

When the adoption fell through, admitting I was furious with God was not enough to resolve my trouble. Only when I began identifying and examining my thoughts about God's character was I challenged with a more truthful interpretation of who God is. Our emotions will naturally flow from what we are thinking, so it is important to challenge any thoughts that are untrue or only partially true.

At the beginning of this chapter, we looked at what Jack was feeling (anger) in response to Mary. But let's take a look at some of Jack's thoughts (see Chart 3.2).

Now we have to ask the question: Were Jack's feelings of hurt, anger, and rage caused by the situation or by Jack's *thoughts* about the situation? Another husband may have had an entirely different way of thinking about his wife's neglecting to put the pens away;

Chart 3.2

Jack's Trouble	Thoughts	Feelings
Mary left the pens out again.	I've told her a million times not to do that.	anger
	She never listens to me.	frustration
	She does it on purpose to annoy me.	irritation
	She doesn't care about me.	pain, sadness
	I have to teach her a lesson she won't forget so she won't do this to me again.	rage

consequently, that husband may have felt and reacted very differently from Jack.

Janice's husband died after a short illness. They had been married only five years, and much of that time had been tumultuous. Things had just started to improve when Ray got sick and died. Janice felt devastated. She struggled with the usual sad feelings of grief and loss, but her grief was compounded by guilt and regret. Let's take a look at Janice's thoughts, as shown in Chart 3.3.

The sad feelings Janice experienced over the death of her husband are perfectly understandable and appropriate. It was true that she would miss him and that her life would forever change. However, we can also see that Janice was experiencing some guilt and regret, deep despair, and other emotions that weren't all related to her loss. Some were related to other thoughts she was having about her situation. In order to deal with her feelings of guilt and regret, Janice would need to examine these thoughts carefully to determine whether each was true, only partially true, or not true at all.

In contrast to Janice, another widow (1 Samuel 25) had a very

Chart 3.3

Trouble	Thoughts	Feelings
death of her husband	I will miss him.	sadness
	I should have done more to show him I loved him.	guilt, regret
	I wasn't a very good wife.	guilt, regret
	I will never be happy again.	despair, unhappiness

different emotional response to the death of her spouse. Abigail was married to Nabal, who is described as a fool. After a drunken rage, Nabal collapsed and died. Let's look at Abigail's response (see Chart 3.4).

Chart 3.4

Trouble	Thoughts	Feelings
death of Nabal	Good, I'm glad God took him.	relief, happiness

Abigail had a very different emotional reaction to the death of her husband. Even in as dramatic a situation as the death of a spouse, our emotional response will be in large part a result of how we think about it.

What We Think Versus What Is True

It is important for us to realize that although our thoughts and feelings are very powerful, they don't always tell us the truth. For example, Zion lamented in Isaiah 49:14, "The LORD has forsaken me, the Lord has forgotten me." We feel deep anguish when we think we have been forgotten and forsaken by the Lord. Although Israel felt and thought those things, God took pains to reassure her that those thoughts were not true. In verses 15 and 16 God replied, "Can a mother forget the baby at her breast and have no compassion on the child she has borne? Though she may forget, I will not forget you! See, I have engraved you on the palms of my hands; your walls are ever before me."

When we feel forgotten by God, it is because we *think* he has forgotten us. But that is not true. We will begin to understand and change our emotional response to our troubles in life when we think truthfully and see the situation as God sees it. Doing this does not remove all unpleasant or painful emotions. Christ's passion in the Garden of Gethsemane is an example of this. Jesus felt real feelings of hurt, betrayal, sadness, and fear. Yet he chose to trust God during the hardest week of his earthly life. We cannot trust with our intellect alone. We must struggle daily to expand our faith beyond our head and into our heart as we learn to believe and trust God completely.

As we discern the truth of our thoughts, we may encounter a variety of thinking errors that misrepresent truth and hinder our process of self-examination.

The Blame Game—It's Your Fault!

Instead of looking at ourselves and our own thoughts and feelings, some of us believe that our feelings are caused by the situation. We say, "You make me nervous." Or, "If only this traffic would clear up, then I wouldn't feel so aggravated." Or, "It's all your fault. If you didn't do this or that, I wouldn't have gotten so mad." Jack, who regularly became furious with his wife, Mary, thought if only she would change her ways, he wouldn't feel so angry and blow up. Jack was convinced that Mary's disorganization caused his angry feelings. He was wrong. Although the things Mary did caused Jack hardship, they did not cause Jack's feelings. If that were true, Jack could never change unless Mary changed first.

We often find it easier to blame others than to look to our own heart for the cause. The blame game is as old as the human race. Adam blamed Eve for his wrong responses, and Eve blamed the serpent. Moses blamed the Israelites when God called him to task for losing his temper. Yet God didn't accept these as excuses, and he held each person accountable for his or her sinful response to the situation. If it's true that others can cause our responses, then why does God hold us accountable for our attitude and behavior? Our responses reflect what is *in* us rather than what has been done *to* us.

Jesus was saddened by his disciples' unbelief. He was hurt by human disrespect and cruelty. But Jesus never blamed others for his responses. His responses to life's problems flowed from who he was and not from what was done to him. In Christ's case, his responses were always pure and right, because they flowed from a sinless heart. In order to mature we need to stop blaming others and to start examining our own heart.

The Entitlement Trap—I Have a Right to Respond This Way

After twenty-six years of marriage to a critical and demanding wife, Bob felt entitled to his feelings of bitterness and hatred. "You don't know what I've had to put up with all these years," he told me. "I have tried to be a good husband, tried to be a godly leader in my home, and all I get is more grief. I don't deserve this kind of marriage. I can't stand her anymore. I want out."

Bob's marriage was a shambles. His wife was an angry, selfish woman who had little capacity to look at her own heart. Bob's response to his wife was understandable, even quite normal, but it was far short of what Jesus wanted to develop in him. Bob's wife was probably never going to change. So what was God trying to do in Bob's heart through this difficult and trying marriage? How could Bob catch a vision for something much more grand than a happy and loving home life with a good woman?

Feeling hurt, betrayed, angry, or sad are normal reactions to mis-treatment and abuse. What we do with those feelings becomes an important decision in our own growth and maturity. We can let them grow and fester like an untended wound that becomes infected and full of pus, or we can acknowledge the wound and move toward forgiveness and healing. As we develop the nature of Christ within, he not only tells us but shows us how to handle the more difficult emotions of hurt, betrayal, mistreatment, and abuse. I never read that Jesus felt glad and rejoiced during those experiences. He hurt as we do. Yet he didn't let his hurt fester into bitterness that caused him to feel hopeless, despairing, or entitled to special treatment. He loved his enemies, prayed for them, and forgave them.

Tim and Joanne lost their only son through the heartless cruelty of another. One evening while Tim Jr. was working at the local grocery store, a robber brutally murdered him for a few dollars. His body was stuffed in the freezer. The murderer was caught, and he confessed to the crime. Tim and Joanne cried. They felt sad, hurt, and broken-hearted. That was normal, but they also felt something else. Instead of responding to the killer with anger and rage, they extended mercy and forgiveness to this man they did not even know. They reached out to the young murderer in prison with the love of God and faithfully visited him in the years following their son's death.

Sometimes we think this kind of love and mercy in the face of hatred and abuse must have been easy for Christ because he was sinless. But the Scripture says Jesus was tempted in every way as we are, and yet was without sin (Hebrews 4:15). Because of this, we may draw near to him with confidence in our time of deepest need.

As a lonely husband, Bob could choose to focus his energies on knowing and loving Christ instead of on trying to have a good and satisfying relationship with his wife. This approach would empower Bob to be more like Christ in forgiving and loving his wife. First Peter 4:19 gives advice to the Christian who is suffering: "So then, those who suffer according to God's will should commit themselves to their faithful Creator and continue to do good."

The Self-Righteous Snare—I'm Right; Therefore, My Response Is Righteous
I hate to admit this, but most of the time in an argument I think I'm right. I argue my point quite well and at times can become very unloving in expressing myself. I don't swear. I don't usually even shout. Yet my self-righteous attitude and tone can drip with contempt as if *my* version of reality is the *only* truth there is.

The pro-life cause has always had a special place in my heart. Perhaps it's because of my personal struggles with trying to have a second baby, but I prefer to believe it's because my heart shares the heart of God on this issue. Maybe it's some of both. I have debated abortion-rights activists on television and college campuses. I have marched in peaceful demonstrations for the cause. I opened my home to an unwed mother. Yet within this movement there are some who believe that just because they are on "God's side" of this issue, their actions (whatever they might be) express the righteous wrath of God.

When we are angry and believe that we are in the right, we need to take care not to excuse or justify a sinful response. The apostle Paul warns us not to sin when we are angry. It is tempting to play God and execute his wrath and judgment whenever we feel our cause is right, whether in the personal or political arena. Our anger, however, just as do all our other emotions, always passes through our sinful heart. So we need to be mindful of how we express ourselves during these times.

The Martyr's Pit—Everything's Fine
Vickey was raised by good people who taught her a deadly lesson. They meant well, but it almost killed her. They taught her never to express any negative emotion or to speak up on her own behalf. "Good Christians, especially good Christian girls, *never* get angry, feel discouraged, or say no!"

Vickey came to counseling on the recommendation of her physician. "Everything is just fine," she smiled, perching on the edge of her seat. "I don't know *why* my doctor thought I needed to see someone."

Probing, I asked about her marriage. "It's great," she said.

"What about your other relationships?"

"Fine."

"Tell me about your walk with Jesus," I asked.

"It's okay." Still perched, still smiling.

"Well, Vickey," I said, "everything in your life seems just perfect. By the way, how's your health?"

"I feel pretty good most of the time," she said, "except for some minor stomach problems I've been having. I have a bleeding ulcer and I'm having trouble eating."

Vickey's body was revealing the secret that Vickey kept hidden so well behind her smile. All was not well in Vickey's life, but she thought that to speak it or even to admit it to herself was a sign of weakness. To do so would mean she was unspiritual and disloyal. Behind Vickey's smiling face were years of stuffed anger and hurt. She could not get access to those emotions as long as her thinking told her that these emotions were not allowed. When she began to let herself *feel*, she realized all was not well at home, with her marriage, with her friendships, or in her spiritual life. Only when she allowed herself to feel those emotions could she gain access to the problems in her life.

THE WAY WE ACT

Jack and Mary responded in different ways to the tension in their marriage. Their thoughts were different and their behaviors were very different. Jack behaved by yelling, belittling, and criticizing Mary, sometimes even shoving and pushing her when he became enraged. Mary didn't act that way during their marital troubles. She withdrew, became fearful and resentful, fell silent, and cried. A. W. Tozer says, "Thinking stirs feeling and feeling triggers action. That is the way we are made and we may as well accept it."[3] (See Chart 3.5.)

As believers, most of us would recognize certain behaviors or actions in Jack's and Mary's life that are wrong or sinful. Jack said that he behaved the way he did because Mary made him so upset. Mary said she behaved the way she did because Jack made her feel so upset.

Just as our feelings flow from our thoughts, our behaviors flow from the combination of our thoughts and feelings. Often everything happens so fast that we don't separate the three. As Christians, we tend to be more aware of sin in the area of our behaviors or actions. When we identify them and try to change only our behaviors without considering the thoughts and feelings that motivate them, we are doomed to repeat the actions and usually fail to achieve any lasting change in our life.

In order to understand ourselves better we must start by taking total responsibility for *our* feelings, *our* thoughts, and *our* actions. We may find it easier to blame these things on our troubles or make other excuses, but if we do, we will not mature. Again, our troubles merely reveal what is already in our hearts.

Chart 3.5

Jack's Trouble	Jack's Actions
Mary's failure to put pens back	blows up, becomes verbally abusive

Mary's Trouble	Mary's Actions
Jack's angry behavior	withdraws, becomes silent

Luke 6:43-45 says, "No good tree bears bad fruit, nor does a bad tree bear good fruit. Each tree is recognized by its own fruit. People do not pick figs from thornbushes, or grapes from briers. The good man brings good things out of the good stored up in his heart, and the evil man brings evil things out of the evil stored up in his heart. *For out of the overflow of his heart his mouth speaks*" (italics mine). Too often we focus on changing our behaviors and give little thought to what is going on in our heart. Thomas à Kempis said, "We must diligently search into and set in order both the outward and the inner man, because both of them are of importance to our progress in godliness."[4] God's purpose in our lives is to glorify himself by restoring his image in us. He uses our troubles in life to help us grow up in him. The cost to us of always believing that our feelings and actions are caused by our troubles is to remain emotionally and spiritually immature.

A potter cannot shape hardened clay. The clay must first be soft and pliable. Only then can the potter mold it with his hands into what he wants it to be. Sometimes we are stiff-necked and unwilling to be worked into his image. For our own good, God sometimes needs to break us, through our troubles, in order to soften our heart and bring it to a place where we can be shaped according to his workmanship, ready to do the good works we were created in him to do (Ephesians 2:10).

THE BEGINNINGS OF CHANGE

As we mature in our faith, we recognize certain responses to troubles as sinful and then seek change. As Jack eventually did, we might seek to hold our tongue, leave the room, or otherwise refrain from express-ing our anger in sinful ways. This is a good first step toward changing our responses, and changing our responses in faithful obedience to God's Word pleases him.

But we need to go deeper if we are to have lasting change in our inner life and not just in our behaviors. We need to challenge our feelings and our thoughts to be more in line with God's perspective. We need to change our feelings by working diligently to interpret the situations we face truthfully. Doing this doesn't always mean changing our negative emotions into positive emotions. Sometimes we will recognize that we are sad or hurt or angry because we face a real loss. At other times we will find that we have perhaps misread a situation or another person. We need to ask ourselves, *Am I seeing the situation correctly? Is there another way to look at it?*

When the adoption fell through, this is how I began. I listened to what I was telling myself. Some of it was true. For example, *I will not be able to adopt this baby, and the birth mother betrayed me.* The painful emotions from those thoughts were difficult enough, but they were based on truth. Further examination revealed my thoughts about God and his character. Those thoughts were lies, yet my anger was real because I *believed* them. Change begins by asking, *Does what I'm telling myself line up with God's Word? Whose perspective is more truthful, mine or God's?*

Next, we move the process from our head to our heart by asking, *Am I going to yield my heart to God's perspective, or will I stubbornly cling to my own version of reality?* This is often the point where we get stuck. Sometimes we are blind or shortsighted and may need help gaining perspective.

While working with Jack and Mary, I helped Jack to examine his thoughts by having him journal each time he felt angry or irritated with Mary over something. I had him create trouble/thought/feeling/behavior charts similar to those in this chapter. This exercise forced Jack to examine some of his irrational thoughts and beliefs. I instructed him to ask himself, *Are these thoughts true? Is there another way of interpreting Mary's behavior?* We can't change our feelings without addressing the thought behind the emotion. And we can't change our behaviors without looking at the thoughts and feelings that go along with them.

If you want to make changes in your life, make a commitment before the Lord to look not only at your sinful behaviors but also at your thoughts and feelings. Begin to take every thought captive to the obedience of Christ (2 Corinthians 10:5). He will reveal the lies you are telling yourself. Sometimes deeper issues will surface that you'll need to work through in order to be freed up to become all that God intends.

Our troubles always bring forth a response from our heart. Becoming mindful of our responses is the second step of the TRUTH Principle. Yet, even when we do this, sometimes we find ourselves stuck in repetitive behaviors, feelings, and thoughts. Jack did manage to control his outbursts better, but he had real trouble letting go of his expectations of Mary. This kept him focused on her instead of on his own maturity, which hindered his growth. The next step of the TRUTH Principle helps us to delve deeper into the hidden motivations of our heart in order to better understand what prevents us from achieving a more lasting change.

TIME FOR REFLECTION

1. Time for self-examination. Start a trouble/thought/feeling/ behavior journal. Begin with your feelings. Identify them and then

put down in your journal the situation or trouble that provoked them. If you are having difficulty with this, start by naming the general feeling category (for example, *sad, mad, hurt, scared, surprised, confused, happy*). Then try to find a word that best describes the intensity of emotion. Next, write down your thoughts about the situation. Journal as many thoughts as come to mind. At this time don't scrutinize them for whether the thoughts are true or rational; just write down whatever you naturally think. Notice how your feelings mirror your thoughts. Then begin to question your thoughts. Are they true? What evidence is there to support your thoughts? Is there another way of looking at the situation? What might be God's perspective of your situation? Last, don't forget to write down how you act in response to your troubles.

2. In what ways have you been blaming others or using the other thinking errors found in this chapter to excuse your sinful responses to your troubles in life? Begin today to take responsibility for your feelings, thoughts, and behaviors in response to your troubles. Read Luke 6:43 carefully, and ask God to show you the things in your heart that fuel these responses.

3. Read Lamentations 3. Create a simple chart. What were Jeremiah's troubles? What were his feelings? What were his thoughts about God and his troubles? Notice in verses 17 and 18 how Jeremiah's feelings mirrored his thoughts. Then notice a shift in Jeremiah's thoughts in verse 21 and the subsequent change in his feelings. The situation never changed! The only thing that changed was Jeremiah's perspective. But that change in thinking made all the difference in how Jeremiah felt about God and the situation he faced. How might a shift of perspective—from your own version of reality to God's perspective—help you respond differently to a difficulty in

your life right now? Ask God to show you the truth. As he shows you the truth, will your heart yield to it? Without your heart involved, your experience of God will remain in your head, and you will not be able to yield a deeper trust in him.

Underlying Idols
of the Heart

As water reflects a face, so a man's heart reflects the man.

As a counselor, I have had many opportunities to speak at conferences and retreats. In the past, this created tremendous anxiety in me. At times I felt physically disabled because of my fear. What was the trouble? What could I do to not be so anxious? Should I claim Philippians 4:6 and pray that God would help me? I did that. Next, I examined my anxious thoughts and challenged them with the truth. After all, what would be the *worst* thing that could happen if I *did* make a fool out of myself? Yet I still battled tremendous physical anxiety. Should I confess my anxiety as sin? I did that—I was still anxious. *What's wrong with me?* I wondered. *Why isn't God's Word working? Why am I not changing?*

These questions are in the hearts of many believers. We pray and read our Bible, but we also stay stuck in repetitive patterns of immaturity and sin. We try to change and perhaps make some progress, but then we fall back to our old familiar ways.

Down through the ages men and women who have attempted to understand the healing of souls have asked two very important questions: "Why do we do what we do?" and "How can we change?" Too often, even as Christians, we have turned to philosophers, secular psychologists, and sociologists for answers. However, I think that these questions are best answered from a theological point of view.

WHY DO WE DO WHAT WE DO?

Answering the question of why we are the way we are is important. Oftentimes we try to blame our past for our current difficulties. Are our troubles the result of what has happened to us? Are they caused by the way we were raised, or by society's cultural disadvantages or ills? Some people who were abused as children or who were otherwise hindered from maturing face significant and legitimate suffering in their adult lives. However, why we are the way we are is much more insidious than what has happened in our past. We do what we do not because of what has happened *to us* but because of what is *in us*.

The familiar story of Adam and Eve is important in understanding the roots of why we act in certain ways. God placed Adam and Eve in the garden. He gave them a wonderful marital relationship in which they were uninhibited with each other. He gave them privilege and responsibility. They were to rule over the animals and work in the lush garden he provided. There was no stress. There was no past baggage or trauma. Their world was perfect, and they were ideally suited to each other. So what went wrong?

Against this perfect backdrop, God asserted his authority and his right to rule his creatures and gave Adam and Eve a command—not to eat the fruit from the tree of knowledge. Next came the test. Would Adam and Eve willingly choose to believe God's ways were best? Would they submit themselves to him? The serpent began his beguiling work on Eve. He challenged God's authority and his right to rule her. Satan did this by appealing to her desires and by calling into question God's character. *It looks good to eat and will give me knowledge like God,* Eve told herself. The tension mounted. Would Eve willingly yield herself to God by obeying him and deny herself what she desired—the fruit that was so appealing?

This is a question we must all face, regardless of our upbringing, our past, our cultural background or whether our life has been advantaged or disadvantaged. *Is God good, and does he have authority in my life and the right to rule me?* Eve sinned because she believed Satan's lies. This caused her to doubt God's goodness and to trust in her own self more than in God. But what was it in Eve that Satan appealed to? Was it her naïveté? This alone would not have caused Eve to sin. Something else was at work. Satan hooked Eve by appealing to her desires.

I have a sweet tooth. Cookies are my downfall. Don't ask me why, but my favorite dessert is chocolate-chip cookies, the hard, crunchy kind. I am not tempted in the least by ginger snaps, vanilla cremes, or Pecan Sandies. Why not? Because I don't desire those kinds of cookies. I love chocolate chips. Cookies with chocolate chips are the ones that tempt me to overindulge. I could easily eat five or six in one sitting.

Temptation can give birth to sin only when it appeals to something already within us that grabs it or attracts it like a magnet. The Bible calls those things that attract temptation our *desires*. Someone once described our desires as the "atomic energy of the soul." They are what give us energy, direction, focus, and pleasure. When Satan successfully takes hold of our desires, whether they be good or sinful, we fall into sin.

Satan appealed to Eve's desire for knowledge and control. She fancied the idea of being like God and having the autonomy and privileges that are associated with being God. In the end, Eve did not willingly yield herself to God's authority. Instead she asserted her desire to rule herself. She wanted to be her own authority and make her own decisions. Adam soon followed suit.

For me, my anxiety around speaking came from a legitimate desire for people to like me and approve of what I had to say. When I feared not getting that and perhaps making a fool of myself, I became anxious. Instead of repenting of my anxiety, I needed to learn how my anxiety was merely a symptom of my pride being threatened (through my desire for approval and praise). Only when I let go of those desires and trusted God for my speaking ministry could I be free from my anxiety. It's not that I don't desire people to like me or my speaking anymore. What's different is that I no longer *need* it in order to be okay. The applause of humankind is not that important to me. Before speaking I check myself for the remnants of anxiety and the fear of man. Those are the clues that my desires are being stimulated. I release those desires to God and speak for his glory and not my own. Then I no longer have to be anxious about my performance.

THREE HINDRANCES TO CHRISTIAN MATURITY

The parable of the sower and the seed (Mark 4) is an important story further illustrating this thought. Jesus describes a farmer who plants seeds. Not all of the seeds that were sown matured into strong and healthy plants that bore fruit. Something hindered or stopped some of the seeds from growing.

The first type of people Jesus describes in this parable are those who hear the Word but do not receive it or take it into their hearts. These people are not interested in a relationship with God. Their hearts are hard. They have no maturity because they have no spiritual life.

The second kind of people described are those who, when they hear the Word, immediately respond in their hearts with joy—but never develop any roots. Remember what happens to the plant with no roots? It dies, never developing flowers or fruit. Fruit is the result of growth and maturity in a plant. A plant cannot mature without healthy roots. Jesus says that the type of faith represented by rootless plants dies as soon as trouble or persecution comes. The faith of some people lacks depth and therefore cannot sustain any growth. They never mature into what Christ intends for them.

The third type of people are those who receive the seed and allow it to take root, but their seeds grow up among thorns, which choke out fruitfulness and deeper maturity. What are these thorns that block growth and development in the Christian's life?

1. Life's Worries

Sally came to counseling emotionally and physically exhausted. She had been told to cut back all her activities, and she knew she should, but she found herself going back to the same overextended routine again and again. She said she wanted to change but found she couldn't. What was the problem for Sally? What was *in* Sally that allowed the temptation to overextend herself to be reignited so that she fell back into familiar patterns?

Sally was a worrier. She was anxious and fearful that if she cut back from all she did, people would be angry with her. That thought was very upsetting for Sally. Even when Sally wired up all her courage to say no to someone's request, if anyone voiced the slightest disappointment in her refusal, she would feel terribly guilty. Sally would brood about how selfish she was and how she should have been able to do more if only she were a better Christian.

What hindered Sally from being all that God wanted her to be?

Her worries. She worried about what others would think of her and feared their disapproval. She felt constant pressure to perform up to everyone's expectations of her, which left little time for her to reflect upon what God really wanted from her.

Sally cannot conquer her problem of being overextended and exhausted by learning to be more assertive or just saying no. She tried that, but when she is tempted to start her doing-routine all over again, Sally finds it hard to resist. In order for Sally to have a deeper change, she will need to look at *why* she does what she does; she will need to identify her *desires*. Not everyone who overextends does so for the same reason. Some people desire to achieve success and fame, but these desires do not grab Sally. She wants something else. Sally wants everyone to be happy with her at all times. She loves it when people like and need her. Sally desires to please people. Until she is able to understand how these desires get so big that they rule her everyday actions, Sally will remain imprisoned with worry in her people-pleasing behaviors and continue to be emotionally and physically exhausted, not to mention spiritually immature.

Although Sally's worries were rooted in people-pleasing desires, other people's worries might stem from different desires. In my case, I sometimes "remind" my adult son about things that, deep down, I am worried about. Did he remember to pay his bill? Did he check on that canceled course he needed to reschedule? I try to control my worry by controlling him. I desire him to be independent and responsible. When that isn't happening as fast as I think it should, I worry. For others, worry might be triggered by a desire to be perfect or a desire for harmony. Jesus tells us that worries (which grow out of our desires that are threatened) will hinder our maturity and growth in Christlikeness.

2. Self-deception

Just like Adam and Eve, God has created us as dependent beings who need him for everything. Saint Augustine says that our soul is restless until it finds rest in him.[1] Yet in our sinful nature, we have been deceived into thinking that we don't really need God. We believe (as Eve believed) that if only we can attain certain things or knowledge, then we won't have to depend wholly on God. We can be sufficient in ourselves.

When we believe our security in life comes from amassing treasures—whether material, social, intellectual, or spiritual—we are deceived. The lie continues when, deep within our heart, we believe that we can be secure and at peace if or when we have enough of whatever we think we need. When our heart believes this lie, it follows that we desire these things. But God warns us against this kind of deception. Isaiah 31:1 says, "Woe to those who go down to Egypt for help, who rely on horses, who trust in the multitude of their chariots and in the great strength of their horsemen, but do not look to the Holy One of Israel, or seek help from the LORD." First Timothy 6:17 instructs us to "Command those who are rich in this present world not to be arrogant nor to put their hope in wealth, which is so uncertain, but to put their hope in God, who richly provides us with everything for our enjoyment."

We deceive ourselves when we rest securely in our riches or in ourselves instead of in God. Perhaps that is why Jesus said that it is easier for a camel to go through the eye of a needle than for a rich man to enter the kingdom of heaven. Even those who are not rich in material wealth can fall prey to this deception. They *desire* wealth and believe that if they had it their lives would be secure. Even without wealth, they fall to the desire for autonomy and security in self and not in God.

3. Other Desires of the Heart

Our inner desires—whether they be good or bad, sinful or not—are the third hindrance to maturity. Anything that competes for God's place in our heart will hinder our growth and fruitfulness. After a couple of counseling sessions, Jack realized that his behavior toward Mary was wrong. He confessed his angry outbursts and abusive behavior as sinful and tried to change. He worked on his thinking, and that helped him not feel so irritated sometimes. But other times he just blew up. He couldn't identify what had happened because it came so fast. Jack was at his wit's end. So was Mary. She felt hopeless that things would ever be different for them. Jack realized that his explosive temper was ungodly. He also acknowledged that his thinking caused his anger more than Mary's behavior. But he still wanted Mary to change. In fact, she *should* change—or so he thought.

I asked Jack, "Right now, what is it that you want from Mary?"

"I just want her to understand me, how upsetting this is for me. She doesn't even try to stop doing those stupid things."

"And when Mary can't or won't stop doing the things that are upsetting to you, Jack, what happens to you?" I prodded.

"I just lose it. I can't stand that she doesn't change. After all, she is supposed to love and submit to me. I'm not asking for anything unreasonable."

Many Christian counselors at this point would turn to Mary and ask her why she doesn't hear Jack's need and accommodate his request. It certainly isn't unreasonable that she try to be more organized around the house. Although this approach is understandable, it would rob Jack of the opportunity to see himself more clearly, and the chance to change and mature.

Jack wanted Mary to change in order to please him and meet his desire for order. The things that Jack desired from Mary—submission, order, understanding, and love—were legitimate, but he allowed those desires to rule his heart. When Jack didn't get what his heart desired, he became furious.

Like Jack, at times we are deceived when what we desire is a good thing. It isn't sinful to want our spouse to understand us, to want our children to obey us, or to want someone to love us. These are legitimate and good desires. The problem arises when our desires become what we want the *most* or think we *need* for life. At that point, legitimate desires become *too* important. They *rule* our heart and stunt the development of the nature of Christ within. God wants us to desire more than anything else to know and be like him. When we let other desires, even good and legitimate ones, take first place in our life, we cannot become like Jesus. Is our heart's desire to please God or to please ourselves? Is our desire to glorify him or to be happy?

A rough paraphrase of James 1:13 says that we are not to blame our sinful reactions on outside temptations or troubles that come our way. We need to understand instead that when troubles or temptations come, they tickle or attract the desires that are already in our heart. The attraction gives birth to sinful desires that rule us.

What's wrong with us? Why do we stay stuck in immaturity, even as Christians? The answer is simple: Because we have not yielded our heart's desires to God's authority, and someone or something other than God is at the helm of our life. Our desires take on a life of their own. Deception is still involved in the process, just as it was in Eden. We are easily deceived because, most of the time, what we want seems so reasonable, so good, and so right. Yet our desires have great potential to mislead and eventually control us.

At a certain marriage retreat, I spoke on "How to Act Right When

Your Mate Acts Wrong." Afterward, one woman asked me how she should respond when her husband neglects to put gasoline in the car and always leaves her with an empty tank. Her usual response to this has been to get angry. She said she prays that God will change her husband and get him to put gas in the tank. She has also prayed that God will stretch the gas in the tank so she won't run out before she has reached her destination. But she still feels furious that her husband is so inconsiderate. I suggested that if her conversations with her husband have fallen on deaf ears, another approach would be to just accept it and make sure she always leaves herself enough time and money to put gas in the car herself. She looked at me wide-eyed and said, "That's not fair! Why should I have to do it?"

She's right; it's not fair. It is only reasonable that her husband should be considerate, and she isn't wrong for desiring consideration and fairness in her marriage. But she is deceived if she thinks she *must* have consideration and fairness in her marriage in order for her to live as Christ would. Then perhaps her desire for these things has become too important and now rules her thoughts and actions, not to mention her emotions.

IDOLS OF THE HEART

Idols are an unfamiliar term to twentieth-century Western Christians. We can picture missionaries dealing with idol worship, perhaps, but not us here in America. God's Word, however, has much to say to us about idols, especially the idols of our heart.

We are designed by God to worship. One definition of worship is "extravagant respect or admiration for or devotion to an object of esteem."[2] In our heart we will worship—or extravagantly admire and devote ourselves to—the things that we love or desire.

Sally devoted herself to pleasing people, for she loved the applause and approval of others. Jack loved control, power, respect, and compliance. When we believe that we *must* have these things in order to have life, we have established an idol to which our heart bows down. "Sin is the outcome of a wrong relationship set up between two of God's creations."[3] Instead of worshiping the Creator, we worship the creature.

Before I knew much about gardening, I planted some orange tiger lilies in the back of my garden. Unfortunately, they were shaded by the overhang on my garage. Each summer I'm amused to watch them strain their long stems and lean in an almost horizontal fashion out from under the overhang, stretching their necks toward the sun. Sometimes in the process their stems break. Flowers are not designed to grow horizontally. They are made to grow straight. Just like my lilies, we lean toward our source of nourishment. If our nourishment is people or things instead of God, we will bend to an unnatural and unhealthy position, damaging the person God designed us to be.

Ezekiel 14:1-5 describes idols of the heart.

> Some of the elders of Israel came to me and sat down in front
> of me. Then the word of the LORD came to me: "Son of man,
> these men have set up idols in their hearts and put wicked
> stumbling blocks before their faces. Should I let them inquire of
> me at all? Therefore speak to them and tell them, 'This is what
> the Sovereign LORD says: When any Israelite sets up idols in his
> heart and puts a wicked stumbling block before his face and
> then goes to a prophet, I the LORD will answer him myself in
> keeping with his great idolatry. I will do this to *recapture the
> hearts* of the people of Israel, who have all deserted me for their
> idols.'" (italics mine)

God desires to transform our heart from a natural person's heart into a spiritual person's heart. God seeks to recapture our heart to return it to him. He wants to be our first love and hates the idols with which we have replaced him. Romans 8:5 says, "Those who live according to the sinful nature have their minds set on what that nature desires; but those who live in accordance with the Spirit have their minds set on what the Spirit desires."

How we act and live stems from what is in our heart. A change of heart requires much more than simply changing sinful behaviors into more Christlike behaviors. A change of heart requires us to allow God to rearrange the desires of our heart. The things that motivate us in our natural self most should no longer control us; instead, the love of Christ should control us, the glory of God should control us, and the mind of Christ should control us.

How do we know if we have idols in our heart? Take them away and watch your reaction. What happens to you when you don't have power and control? When you don't have peace and serenity? When you don't have pleasure or approval? When you don't have respect or security? When you don't have a fat bank account? When you are not recognized for your accomplishments? When you are ignored or humiliated? What happens to you when you don't get your way? We often don't know our heart is so attached to our idols until they're threatened. Then we fight like mad to keep them!

James 4 describes the source of conflict among people. James says it is the result of not getting what we want. Our wants or desires, when they take first place in our life, will always interfere with our relationship with God and usually with our relationship with others. God, in his great love for us, always seeks to detach our affections from anything that takes preeminence over him in our hearts. "For where your treasure is, there your heart will be also" (Matthew 6:21). He wants and deserves first place!

Our God-created disposition is that of a dependent creature. Yet since Eve we have rebelled against that truth. We have wanted to be our own god or make our own god. Oswald Chambers says, "Sin…is not wrong doing, it is wrong *being*, deliberate and emphatic independence of God."[4]

God is a jealous God. He is jealous of our love. When we love things more than we love him, he hates it. Ephesians 5 says that when we love something, we will nourish and care for it. When we love our idols, we embrace them, love them, devote ourselves to them, and make it our business to please them, whether they be our love of approval, love of money, love of success, love of being right, love of ourselves, love of plea- sure, or love of people. We also live in bondage to our fears, such as the fear of conflict, fear of failure, fear of disapproval, fear of rejection, fear of humiliation, or fear of intimacy. Our fears are a helpful way of look- ing at the other side of what we love. For example: We love success; we fear failure. We love peace; we fear conflict. We love to please people and make them happy; we fear their disapproval or rejection.

Second Kings 17:40-41 offers a sad commentary on the children of Israel that I'm afraid applies to many of us as well. "They would not lis- ten, however, but persisted in their former practices. Even while these people were worshiping the LORD, they were serving their idols. To this day their children and grandchildren continue to do as their fathers did."

HOW CAN WE CHANGE?

Jesus told us in Mark 12:30 that the most important commandment is to "love the Lord your God with all your heart and with all your soul and with all your mind and with all your strength." Do we really love God that much? What do you love the *most?* For many of us, our other loves are not bad loves, they're just out of order. We love good things, but we love them too much—more than we love God. What we love *rules* our heart.

When we love God, he is infinitely patient with our awkwardness and mistakes in expressing that love. On the other hand, he hates when we pretend we love him while our hearts are attached to something else. He calls that spiritual adultery (Jeremiah 3; James 4:4).

Fénelon, a wise servant of God, warns us: "Do not be surprised at the sternness of his jealousy. Of what then is he so jealous? Is it of our talents, intelligence, the regularity of outer virtues? No. He is condescending and easy about all such things. Love is jealous only of love."[5] We commit spiritual adultery by allowing other loves to control our heart and life instead of the love of God and the love for God.

What did Jack love the most that kept him from really changing his life? He loved power and control. He loved getting his way. He loved himself. When Jack looked at his angry temper as the problem, he was not looking at his main problem. His temper was a problem for Mary, but his temper was a symptom of the real problem for Jack: his idols. He loved having power, having control, being right, and getting his own way much more than he loved Mary or even the Lord. Until Jack repents of loving other things more than he loves God and his wife, he won't be able to get a consistent grip on his temper.

What about Sally? Sally loved pleasing people and feared their disapproval. Sally loved being needed. Sally won't be able to change her people-pleasing behavior unless she begins to love Jesus more than she loves approval.

God longs for our love as a bridegroom longs for his bride's love and devotion. Sadly, what we often do is pretend to love God when we merely want to enjoy the pleasures of his love. We love being loved but do not press on to maturity in loving God.

What rules your heart? What we love the most will rule us. Or to put it another way, what we most fear losing will control us. God says he is a jealous God and he wants to be first in our heart. Many of us repent of wrong behaviors, even wrong thoughts, but we don't understand that we can't grow to be more like Christ unless our heart loves something more passionately than we love ourselves—or our own desires.

CONSEQUENCES OF OUR IDOLATRY

The Bible mentions some serious consequences for idolatry. Jonah 2:8 says "Those who cling to worthless idols forfeit the grace that could be theirs." We will always forsake a deeper walk with God when we cling to those things that we love more than we love him. Trusting God and loving him involves giving him the desires of our heart. When we delight ourselves in him, he does give us the desires of our heart—because the desires of our heart are his desires for us. God doesn't despise good things in our lives. We just need to make sure that we don't want them the *most*. In this step of the TRUTH Principle we expose the idols of our heart and begin the process of change. Setting our heart in order is making sure that we have submitted our heart—our affections, our mind, and our desires—to the things that God says are good and right. We have given him the right to rule us. He is at the center of our heart because he *is* the desire of our heart.

Litany of Humility

O Jesus, meek and humble of heart,

Make our heart like Yours.

From the desire of being esteemed,

DELIVER ME, O JESUS.

From the desire of being loved,

From the desire of being extolled,

From the desire of being honored,

From the desire of being praised,

From the desire of being preferred,

From the desire of being consulted,

From the desire of being approved,

From the desire of being popular,

From the fear of being humiliated,

From the fear of being despised,

From the fear of suffering rebukes,

From the fear of being calumniated,

From the fear of being forgotten,

From the fear of being wronged,

From the fear of being ridiculed,

From the fear of being suspected,

That others may be loved more than I,

JESUS, GRANT ME THE GRACE TO DESIRE IT

That others may be esteemed more than I,

That in the opinion of the world, others may increase and I

may decrease,

That others may be chosen and I set aside,

That others may be praised and I unnoticed,

That others may be preferred to me in everything.

That others may become holier than I, provided that I may
become as holy as I should....
Lamb of God, who takes away the sins of the world, have
mercy on us, O Lord.[6]

TIME FOR REFLECTION

1. Part of the self-examination process that we started in chapter 3 will be to look for your idols. The next time you're upset, ask yourself not only what you are feeling and thinking but what you want. Do you want to be happy? Do you want to be understood? Do you want to be free from stress? Do you desire people to like you? Are you wanting good grades? Do you desire obedient children? When you've identified what you want, are you willing to lay it down for Jesus? Do you believe that if he doesn't allow you to have the desire of your heart, it is because he loves you and that his heart knows what is best for you? If he chooses not to allow you to have what you want, are you willing to yield that decision to him in faith?

2. Read Jesus' exhortation to the church in Ephesus in Revelation 2. He said she did many good things and followed the *rules*, but had lost her first love. Maybe that's been a picture of your Christian life. What has been the deepest desire of your heart? Is the love of God and the love for God controlling you and ordering your life? Or have you found that other desires, even legitimate and good ones, have crept into first place? What are they?

3. In chapter 1 we were reminded that our love for God grows out of our understanding and experience of his love for us. Spend some time with God meditating on his love for you. A good place to begin would be to focus on the Cross. Romans 5:8 says, "But God *demonstrates* his own love for us in this: While we were still sinners, Christ died for us" (italics mine).

Read Ephesians 3:17-19. Paul prays that we would be rooted and established in the love of God.

4. For further study take a concordance and look up the word *desire.* Read through all the verses that talk about our desires and how they rule us and control us in the natural man. After coming to Christ, the Scripture teaches us that we are to develop new desires.

List what the desires of the natural man are. Note the difference between evil desires and desires that are good but that have gotten too important. Begin to consciously yield your desires to God that he might have his way with you.

CHAPTER FIVE

TRUTH: THE MIRROR TO OUR HEART

Sanctify them by the truth; your word is truth.

JOHN 17:17

One Sunday after church my husband and I drove home in a pounding rainstorm. Our son, Ryan, was strapped snugly in his car seat. It was past his lunchtime and he was hungry—starving, from his perspective. Loud wails and giant tears told us what we already knew. He was deeply distressed and very unhappy with us. How could we just sit there and do nothing? At only six months of age, although he couldn't speak, his eyes communicated clearly to me: "Mommy, why don't you care about me? I'm hurting and I'm hungry. How can you just sit by and watch me suffer?"

At that moment in time, Ryan's limited perception of reality was truth for him. To him, we didn't care. We didn't love him. We were impervious to his cries for relief. Yet there was something Ryan didn't know and I couldn't communicate. Because it was dangerous, I didn't scoop him out of his car seat and snuggle him to my breast. The road was slick and visibility was bad. I didn't want to take a chance on getting in an accident. I just wanted to get safely home. A reality bigger than Ryan was able to grasp applied to the situation. It was beyond him, and I couldn't even explain it to him. He was too little to understand.

In the midst of my maternal distress God softly spoke to my heart: *This is what happens with you, Leslie. When you are screaming and hollering at me and you think I don't hear you or I don't care, that's not true. It's just that you don't understand my ways. You are too little (or immature) to grasp what I am doing or why.* God said, "For my thoughts are not your thoughts, neither are your ways my ways.... As the heavens are higher than the earth, so are my ways higher than your ways and my thoughts than your thoughts" (Isaiah 55:8-9).

OUR HEARTS ARE PRONE TO DECEPTION

As humans, our pride can deceive us into thinking that we are the source of our own truth. Before the fall, our reason, logic, intuition, imagination, and emotions were all calibrated to grasp true reality. After the fall, our nature became sinful, and all of our abilities are now flawed, tainted, and damaged (Jeremiah 17:9). Just like my son who couldn't grasp the truth of the situation because of his limitations, we cannot discern truth or reality apart from God.

While attending college, I was active in the ministry of Campus Crusade for Christ. Perhaps on college campuses more than anywhere else, people's reason and intellect often interfere with their coming to know Christ. "How could you honestly believe that Christ was born of a virgin?" one college student chided. "It isn't possible to be raised from the dead," another sneered. "To become a Christian means I have to put my brains on the shelf."

These miracles are impossible, according to human reason and logic. But God tells us that human intellect and reason are limited and can deceive us when they become our ultimate source of truth and reality. Psalm 14:1 says, "The fool says in his heart, 'There is no God.'" And Isaiah 47:10: "You have trusted in your wickedness and have said, 'No one sees me.' Your wisdom and knowledge mislead you when you say to yourself, 'I am, and there is none besides me.'"

When we are our own source of ultimate truth, our heart is prone to lulling us into a false sense of security and trust in the wrong things. The prophets warned the people of Israel not to fall into this trap of false security—judgment is coming, they said. (See, for example, Isaiah 32:9-14.)

Not only is human reason flawed, our intuition and imagination can deceive us and even cause us to question our own logic. Tom came for counseling full of fear, afraid he was going to die. He described various physical aches and pains that he thought were catastrophic illnesses. His doctor sought to reassure him that all was well, but Tom would not believe him. Tom also struggled with a fear of fires. Every night before retiring he would check all the electrical outlets and appliances in his home to make sure they were off. But as soon as he lay down to sleep, his mind would begin to race. He would imagine that he had forgotten to shut something off. This thought would generate a picture of a fire burning out of control and of people dying. He would remind himself that he had indeed unplugged everything, but his imagination would continue to run wild until he got up again to check. This routine could continue for hours. Tom's imagination was competing with his reason and logic, and neither could provide him any reassurance of the truth.

Our senses can also deceive us. They can trick us into believing that temporal pleasures bring joy and delight to our soul. We can be deceived into believing that something bad for us (like drugs, illicit sexual relationships, or pornography) is good. It *feels* so good. Our senses register it as pleasing and fun. We justify and rationalize it to our minds. Yet in the end God says it will ruin us. "He feeds on ashes, a deluded heart misleads him; he cannot save himself, or say, 'Is not this thing in my right hand a lie?'" (Isaiah 44:20).

The apostle Paul describes this process in the first chapter of his epistle to Romans. He says that by nature we suppress the truth of God and, in our sinfulness, we exchange the truth of God for a lie. As fallen people we do this automatically and naturally. Often it is not a conscious thought or decision. "Sin originated in the darkening of the human mind and heart as man turned from the truth about God to embrace a lie about him and consequently a whole universe of lies about his creation. Sinful thoughts, words and deeds flow forth from this darkened heart automatically and compulsively, as water from a polluted fountain."[1]

I am often struck by the enormity of self-deception that people naturally engage in. Working with those who have experienced abuse at the hands of their parents has given me a bird's-eye view not only of the lies of the enemy, but also of the ways children naturally exchange the truth for lies.

Carla was sexually molested by her father from the age of five. Much of the work that Carla had to do in counseling was not around what had happened to her (although it was sinful and terrible) but what Carla *did* with what happened to her. From the beginning of the molestation, Carla attempted to make sense of what was happening to her. Why was her daddy hurting her? Carla began to answer her questions with conclusions that made perfect sense to a five-year-old mind but were in reality a jumble of confusing lies.

Carla told herself that she must have been a very bad girl for her father to do this to her. She believed God was angry with her for allowing her father to touch her without stopping him or telling someone. Carla also told herself she was a sick person for enjoying some of the attention that she received from her father during the molestation.

Much of Carla's work in therapy involved learning to identify and undo the lies she had told herself about the molestation and putting the experience under the light of God's truth. That was her only source of healing. If Carla's natural heart exchanged the truth of God for a lie, then what was the truth? What does God say about what happened to Carla? The truth is that God loves children. Carla was a precious gift to her parents. God hates what Carla's father did. Naturally she would enjoy special attention from her father—all little girls do. The truth is that she was the victim and he was the perpetrator. As painful as it was for Carla to admit, the truth from God's perspective was that her father spitefully used his position of power and influence in her life for his own selfish purposes. What he did hurt Carla terribly. Only by facing the truth could she begin to experience healing and be set free from the devastating effects of childhood sexual abuse.

Both Tom and Carla were deceived into believing false things about themselves and their situations. Similarly, we can deceive ourselves into believing false things about God. Ann thought she had committed the unpardonable sin. Unmarried and pregnant, she had an abortion. She believed that God could not forgive her. Guilt and sorrow overwhelmed her. Her weight dropped and she couldn't sleep. When presented with the good news that Jesus forgives sins, even big ones, Ann remained unmoved. She knew that's what God said, but in her heart, she wouldn't believe him. She exchanged God's truth for the lie that abortion is *so* bad it is unforgivable.

On the other hand, Susan was convinced that God was in favor of her abortion. She believed that God wanted her to be financially secure and happily married before bringing any children into the world. Because she was neither secure nor happy, Susan deceived herself into believing that God endorsed her decision to abort her unborn child.

In the January-February 1998 issue of *Treating Abuse Today*, there was an article describing some of the philosophy of the North American Man/Boy Love Association (NAMBLA). NAMBLA purports that sexual relations between adult men and boys is good. They believe that it is only harmful because society has negative prejudices against it.[2] Our minds can deceive us into thinking that we are doing good things when in reality we are doing very bad things. God says, "Woe to those who call evil good and good evil, who put darkness for light and light for darkness, who put bitter for sweet and sweet for bitter" (Isaiah 5:20).

In our culture, the individual has become the ultimate source of truth. Since the period of enlightenment during the eighteenth century, we have emphasized the individual and the ability of the individual to use his own reason and thinking as a final source of truth. As a culture, we have come to define truth internally (i.e., what I think or feel is true or right) rather than to define it externally with the Scriptures or the church.[3] We have all heard the statement, "It may be true for you, but it's not true for me." Our culture has lost confidence in objective truth apart from one's own sense of knowing something. Perhaps that is why many Christians describe a schism between their heart and their head. They know what God says is true, but their own sense of things doesn't quite believe it.

Jesus describes Satan as "the father of lies" (John 8:44, NASB). His objective has always been to confuse people about what is true. He seeks to destroy us by accusing us of our sins (Revelation 12:10) and by causing our heart to doubt God and to believe that something other than God will bring us life. He deceived Eve by causing her to doubt God's goodness and his plan for her. She sinned when she doubted God's ability to lovingly rule her life and began to trust her own sense of things. What is true and real can never be fully discerned by looking to self for the answers. We are vulnerable to being misled, confused, or deceived. God reminded Israel through Jeremiah the prophet that he had instructed their forefathers, "Obey me, and I will be your God and you will be my people. Walk in all the ways I command you, that it may go well with you." But as we learn in the following verse, "they did not listen or pay attention; instead, they followed the stubborn inclinations of their evil hearts. They went backward and not forward" (Jeremiah 7:23-24).

WHERE CAN WE FIND TRUTH?

"One of the roots of mental illness is invariably an interlocking system of lies we have been told and lies we have told ourselves."[4] Only through knowing the truth can we begin to bring light upon the dark places in our hearts. Ultimate truth, or true reality, which I discussed in chapter 2, will never be found in human knowledge or experience. Truth is much bigger than that. Truth isn't something we learn; truth is *Someone* we know.

Jesus said that he is the Truth (John 14:6) and that he was telling the truth. In the Gospels, Jesus said, "I tell you the truth" more than seventy times. Jesus prayed that we would be sanctified (or changed) by the truth, and he confirmed God's Word as truth (John 17:17).

Psalm 119 is filled with the psalmist's overwhelming commitment to follow God's Word as truth. The psalmist prays, "Keep me from deceitful ways; be gracious to me through your law. I have chosen the way of truth" (Psalm 119:29-30).

God and his Word are our only source of objective truth. "I am the LORD your God, who teaches you what is best for you" (Isaiah 48:17). The human intellect is incapable of grasping the eternal God. It must give way to faith, which is superior to intellect or reason. "Faith is the ladder that leads us to the vantage point from whence we can behold, through a glass darkly, the deep things of God."[5] When our reason, logic, emotions, intuitions, or imaginations conflict with what God says, who are we going to believe? Who are we going to trust? Eve fell into sin because she believed what the serpent said rather than what God told her. God wants us to believe *him*, not just to believe *in* him. He longs for our trust, even in the face of contradictory evidence. The simplest definition of faith is found in Genesis 15:6: "Abram believed the LORD, and he credited it to him as righteousness." God and the Scriptures are our source of truth. Hebrews 6:18-19 tells us that God doesn't lie, and we have this assurance as an anchor for our soul.

THE TRUTH ABOUT HUMANITY

One day during a counseling session Amber said, "You know, I really don't like that song 'Amazing Grace.'"

"Oh?" I replied, curious as to why.

"I don't like that word *wretch*. I'm not a wretch!"

"Today, we live the lie that we are 'pretty good' people who occasionally 'make mistakes.'"[6] Because of this mind-set, we hate seeing our flaws and imperfections, not to mention the horror of our deepest sins.

For those of us who wrestle with our weight, we avoid stepping on the scale or looking in a full-length mirror after our shower. We'd rather not know the truth.

In the same vein, many of us struggle with being open before God and his Word. The psalmist cried, "Search me, O God, and know my heart; test me and know my anxious thoughts. See if there is any offensive way in me, and lead me in the way everlasting" (Psalm 139:23-24). God is light, and it is in the light of his presence that we see ourselves truthfully. But many of us flee truth tellers like scales and mirrors, and we don't spend time in God's presence asking him to reveal to us our heart. As long as we don't put ourselves under the light of God's Spirit and his Word, we will remain ignorant or deceived about our true condition.

I'm reminded of a story about a woman all dressed up for a party in a beautiful white dress. As she got out of her automobile, a passing car splashed water on her. Thinking that the water droplets would soon evaporate, the woman continued walking toward the house where the party she was to attend was in full swing. To her dismay, as she approached the bright lights of the home's foyer, she realized that she had not been splashed with clear water that would evaporate, but with brown, muddy water. Only when she came under the light of another —in this case the house—did she see her true condition.

Jesus is Truth, and Truth changes people's hearts and lives. Knowing truth is "to line up with the way things really are."[7] Being in a relationship with Jesus is a process of allowing yourself to be examined by God's Word and God's Spirit. "You have set our iniquities before you, our secret sins in the light of your presence" (Psalm 90:8). If truth does not enter our heart and cause us to repent and to love and obey God more, then it is mere theological intellectualism.

Jesus shows us the path to a fulfilling life. He says, "If anyone would come after me, he must deny himself and take up his cross and follow me. For whoever wants to save his life will lose it, but whoever loses his life for me will find it. What good will it be for a man if he gains the whole world, yet forfeits his soul?" (Matthew 16:24-26). The world teaches us just the opposite. It teaches us that the way to a fulfilling life is to satisfy self and to make ourselves happy. Whom will we trust? We only have one life to live. We cannot follow after both God and self.

Traditionally we have considered Jesus' statement from a limited perspective, that he is talking about losing our soul to eternal damnation. But I believe the question Jesus is asking is larger than that. He asks us to consider this: What can we possibly gain in life by striving after things that will ultimately result in the loss of everything? For the word *soul* is not merely spiritual; it is our essence—who we are, not just in eternity but now. It refers to what we were originally created to be—in other words, our true self. Our soul is us, and we have been created for relationship with God, to love him and enjoy him *forever*. Our true soul longs to be connected to God. When we are united with God we reach our fullest potential as human beings, which is to bring him glory. Yet in our stubborn self-deceptiveness and rebellion, we connect our soul instead to everything that is false—the idols of our heart.

The story of the rich young ruler (Mark 10:17-22) provides a good example of someone who is unaware and deceived. In this story the young man asks Jesus what *good* thing he needs to do to get eternal life. Jesus tells him that there is only One good, but he should obey the commandments. The young man wants to know specifically which commandments to obey. He already knows that he keeps the commandments; he's trying to show Jesus that he is good. Knowing what this young man is up to, Jesus begins the process of exposing his heart. Jesus says, "Do not murder, do not commit adultery, do not steal, do not give false testimony, do not defraud, honor your father and mother" (Mark 10:19). The young man says he has all those commands covered. "Is there anything else?" he asks. This is where Jesus zeroes in on the young man's heart and brings him to the light of truth.

The account tells us that "Jesus looked at him and loved him" (v. 21). The truth was that Jesus desired to be in a relationship with that young man, but the young man was focused on keeping the rules. Jesus knew his heart. He said, "One thing you lack. Go, sell everything you have and give to the poor, and you will have treasure in heaven. Then come, follow me." When the young man heard this, "he went away sad, because he had great wealth" (v. 22).

Rules don't change us, Jesus does. Jesus told that young man that the one commandment he failed to keep was the first and most important one. "Love the Lord your God with all your heart and with all your soul and with all your mind and with all your strength" (Mark 12:30). Jesus revealed this young man's other loves to him when he told him to sell all his possessions. When the young man walked away, he confirmed what Jesus already knew was in his heart—it was his wealth, not his love for God. That young man would not deny himself in order to know and love Jesus. The saddest part of the whole story is that he kept his money but lost himself.

God always wants first place in our heart. God's truth is addressed not just to our intellect but to our heart, where our will resides. To follow God's truth is not to mentally agree with it; it is to radically obey and follow it. It changes the way we live. Our will is our internal rudder, steering us toward what we think and feel we need the most for life. It moves us toward what our reason, emotions, and senses have determined to be the good and best things. These in turn will determine what we will love and what we will worship. Without God's truth guiding our reason, logic, imagination, and feelings, these will always be idols. We need to submit ourselves—our intellect and reason, our imagination, intuition, and emotions—to the authority and guidance of God's truth. Remember, God has created us to enjoy him forever. Life is found in him, and we are to become like him. Anything less is death of our true self, in this life and in the next. God loves to know we desire *him* more than anything else (Psalm 42:1; Psalm 73:25).

The fact that an airplane can fly in total darkness has always amazed me. The pilot must rely on his instruments and not on his logic or on his own sense of sight, balance, or hearing. He trusts in a greater truth or reality beyond his perception to guide the plane. To refuse would mean disaster. But a pilot doesn't learn to use his instruments for guidance overnight. He has training and practice to use these tools, learning to trust them to guide him through even the blackest night.

As Christians we, too, need to learn to trust someone greater than ourselves to guide us. We are not capable of seeing or knowing all truth, but there is One who is. "Trust in the LORD with all your heart and lean not on your own understanding; in all your ways acknowledge him, and he will make your paths straight" (Proverbs 3:5-6).

PRACTICING THE PRESENCE OF GOD

Believing by faith is one level of the Christian journey; walking by faith is another. "Blessed are those who have learned to acclaim you, who walk in the light of your presence, O LORD" (Psalm 89:15). If we are to enter into our truest and greatest capacity as human beings, we need to enter into another dimension of reality that is not common to human experience. Jesus showed us the way. He lived daily in God-centered reality, and when he was taken up to heaven, he promised he would give us the Spirit of truth, assuring us that God's presence would reside within us (John 14:16-17).

Practicing the presence of God in its simplest terms means yielding ourselves to the authority of God and being mindful of the spiritual realm around us. It means we allow the Holy Spirit to teach us to see everything from God's perspective. Mother Teresa practiced the presence of God and was empowered to work with the poorest of the poor in Calcutta. Each day she would spend hours in prayer to prepare her heart for the work. Thus she became able to see people with a different set of eyes. She saw them as "Jesus in His distressing disguise"[8] just as the Scriptures tell us that "whatever you did for one of the least of these brothers of mine, you did for me" (Matthew 25:40).

A recent craze among teens is What-Would-Jesus-Do (WWJD) jewelry. Practicing the presence of God does mean understanding and trying to do what Jesus would do, but it is more than that. Practicing the presence of God means daily processing the reality of our experience with the truth of who God is and what he says. It means growing to understand the mind of God—how God thinks, feels, and what he wants. It means living in sync with our Creator and using each moment to live out our purpose.

Stephen Covey tells of an experience he had one Sunday morning while riding a subway in New York.

People were sitting quietly—some reading newspapers, some lost in thought, some resting with their eyes closed. It was a calm, peaceful scene.

Then suddenly, a man and his children entered the subway car. The children were so loud and rambunctious that instantly the whole climate changed.

The man sat down next to me and closed his eyes, apparently oblivious to the situation. The children were yelling back and forth, throwing things, even grabbing people's papers. It was very disturbing. And yet, the man sitting next to me did nothing.

It was difficult not to feel irritated. I could not believe that he could be so insensitive as to let his children run wild like that and do nothing about it, taking no responsibility at all. It was easy to see that everyone else on the subway felt irritated, too. So finally, with what I felt was unusual patience and restraint, I turned to him and said, "Sir, your children are really disturbing a lot of people. I wonder if you couldn't control them a little more?"

The man lifted his gaze as if to come to a consciousness of the situation for the first time and said softly, "Oh, you're right. I guess I should do something about it. We just came from the hospital where their mother died about an hour ago. I don't know what to think, and I guess they don't know how to handle it either."

"Suddenly," Covey writes, "I *saw* things differently, and because I *saw* differently, I *thought* differently, I *felt* differently, I *behaved* differently. My irritation vanished. I didn't have to worry about controlling my attitude or my behavior; my heart was filled with the man's pain. Feelings of sympathy and compassion flowed freely.... Everything changed in an instant."[9]

When the curtain went up and Covey saw the larger truth of the situation, the irritation he had been experiencing just moments before vanished, and his heart filled with compassion for the young father and his family. Knowing the whole story changed him. Oswald Chambers says prayer doesn't always change the situation, prayer changes us.[10] Practicing the presence of God means learning to stay tuned to God so that we might continually see life from his perspective.

Sarah sat crying out to the Lord, "Why?" Her husband had left her for a younger woman, and she was devastated and frightened. She had no job skills. She had no income of her own. She felt all alone. Yet sitting still in the presence of God renewed her strength. She said, "I could think about the same things I thought of earlier that day, but this time I felt differently. The pain wasn't as deep as before. Somehow, I knew that God would walk me through it." Practicing the presence of God doesn't remove us from life's difficult circumstances; it just puts them into perspective and gives us the strength to walk through them—like Jesus did.

Faithfully practicing the presence of God helps us remember what is true. The blockbuster movie *Titanic* vividly portrayed people who didn't keep this in perspective. The ship was mortally wounded and sinking. Yet many people both ignored the warning signals and gaily pretended not to know what deep in their hearts they did know—that death was coming. Instead of preparing to enter eternity, they danced. Practicing the presence of God helps us remember the truth about ourselves, the world, and sin. It keeps us mindful that while the band is playing, people are laughing, and everyone *looks* happy, the ship (the world we live in) is sinking.

As humans we are forgetful people. The Scripture consistently speaks of man's tendency to forget God. The things of the world have a way of distracting us and giving us spiritual amnesia. We forget who we really are and what we are really here for. Many of us live as if this life is all there is, as if our main task is to make ourselves happy. Staying in the presence of God keeps our spiritual side alert, aware of true reality and the larger picture around us so we don't live our lives merely on the temporal plane.

Practicing the presence of God gives us peace. The psalmist says, "Be still before the LORD and wait patiently for him; do not fret when men succeed in their ways, when they carry out their wicked schemes" (Psalm 37:7). Stilling our heart in God's presence helps us stay centered on what is true, good, and right instead of being carried away by our fears, our lusts, or our desires.

Many verses reassure us of God's unfailing love for his people and his commitment to us. God is holy and good. He is sovereign. Nothing comes to us without his consent. Therefore as we center our hearts in the presence of God, we can know that he is running the show and we need not fret. Psalm 16:8 says, "I have set the LORD always before me. Because he is at my right hand, I will not be shaken." Fénelon says, "The practice of the presence of God is the supreme remedy. It sustains. It comforts. It calms."[11]

The psalmist declares, "You have made known to me the path of life; you will fill me with joy in your presence, with eternal pleasures at your right hand" (Psalm 16:11). Ultimately, the human soul will be transformed to a state that loves God and enjoys him forever. Eternally enjoying the presence of God is heaven. We get tastes of heaven when we practice his presence while we are still confined to earth. We also get tastes of hell when we don't know or experience the presence of God. Hell is separation from God for all of eternity.

Faith uses the imagination to ponder what God has already

promised (Hebrews 11). These promises become the foundation for our trust in him. We don't always receive the promises in their entirety, but we believe they are coming, and that is enough for now. Only in eternity will we see the whole picture of what God is making of our lives in human history. Meanwhile, we walk by faith, not by sight, reason, emotion, or sheer will power. Sometimes God opens the curtain and gives us fleeting glimpses of something more. Those moments give us a taste of a life beyond what we know, a taste that causes our souls to hunger for higher ground. These experiences come through good times and bad and remind our true self that this world is not our home. Our true home will be more beautiful and glorious than we could possibly imagine. The apostle Paul tells us, "We've been given a glimpse of the real thing, our true home, our resurrection bodies! The Spirit of God whets our appetite by giving us a taste of what's ahead. He puts a little of heaven in our hearts so that we'll never settle for less" (2 Corinthians 5:4-5, MSG).

TIME FOR REFLECTION

1. What is your picture of God? How have you heard his voice in the past? Is your picture of God the same one described in the Scriptures? What is your ultimate source for truth about God, the Bible, or your own sense of things?

2. Take a minute to reflect on these biblical truths:

- God is a personal God who loves me with a passionate love.

- God longs to redeem us so we are not separate from him.
- God desires to separate us from anything that hinders our relationship with him.
- God desires to restore our souls—to reflect his image in us.

As you meditate on these truths, does your heart believe them? If not, what hinders you from believing God? Begin to ask God to increase your faith so that you might believe him and trust him more.

3. Psalm 139:23-24 says, "Search me, O God, and know my heart; test me and know my anxious thoughts. See if there is any offensive way in me, and lead me in the way everlasting." Ask God to reveal his truth about you.

> The most effective kind of prayer is that in which we place our-selves, in our hearts, before God, relinquishing all resistance, let-ting go of all secret irritation, opening ourselves to the truth, to God's holy mystery, saying over and over again, "I desire truth, I am ready to receive it, even this truth which causes me such concern, if it be the truth. Give me the light to know it—and to see how it bears on me." (Romano Guardini)[12]

4. Meditate on Psalm 119. Pray and journal through each section. When the psalmist mentions the word *truth,* stop and ask yourself if you are allowing God's word to mold you. Do you want to know things as God sees them or just your version of reality? Are your thoughts, values, beliefs, behaviors, goals, desires, dreams, hopes, and aspirations lining up with the truth? Or do you mold God's word and use it for your purposes?

5. Begin to set aside time each day to practice the presence of God. Read Psalm 25:4-5. He is always with us and in us. Practicing

his presence makes us more aware of him and builds our trust in him. "We can achieve this sense of God's presence by surrendering our hearts and wills to Him, and through the conscious choice to make ourselves aware of Him throughout the day. We can learn to pray simultaneously with the other activities of our days, letting prayer season everything we do. If practiced regularly in this manner, prayer becomes as natural and integral to us as drawing our next breath."[13]

CHAPTER SIX

OUR HEART'S RESPONSE TO GOD'S TRUTH

*The solution to indwelling sin in the believer
involves both a divine work and a human response.*

JOHN D. HANNAH

One of my greatest joys as a Christian counselor is watching God work in a heart and in a home. Sometimes I marvel how God has given me a box seat in the daily dramas that unfold before me. One such story I'd like to share is Jared and Isobel's.

Isobel came to counseling over troubles in her marriage and with her adult children. Her two grown daughters and their children had recently moved back home, and their presence was creating a lot of tension between Isobel and her husband, Jared. She often felt at her wit's end struggling to be a mediator between her husband and their daughters. Each of them accused her of taking sides. After working, taking care of home responsibilities, and baby-sitting the grandchildren, Isobel found little time to relax or enjoy life. She sensed Jared withdrawing from her and from the Lord. In fact, she was afraid he might be involved with another woman, and one awful night Jared confessed.

He had been in an adulterous relationship. Isobel's world crashed down around her. Jared wasn't sure he wanted to stay married. He didn't know if he loved Isobel anymore, and he didn't know what to do.

Isobel began the arduous task of self-examination. It would have been tempting to focus on Jared and his sin, but instead she started by looking at some of the reasons why Jared had begun to drift away from her. As she began to understand her role in the chain of events, she confessed to her husband the ways in which she had failed to love him. Her words did not absolve him of his choice to have an affair, but they opened the lines of communication just a little bit, and Jared agreed to come to counseling.

Jared hated what he had done. He ended the relationship with the other woman but still felt stuck. "I just don't know how to get that feeling back for Isobel," Jared shared. Meanwhile, Isobel continued deepening her relationship with God through prayer. She leaned on God as she never had before. She didn't know what would happen, but she knew that God loved them and was in control. She made a conscious decision to forgive Jared and to work toward reconciling their marriage. Jared struggled with both accepting what he had done and receiving Isobel's and God's forgiveness. Week by week, God was at work.

Just before Christmas, the three of us were chatting about getting all our Christmas shopping done when Jared said, "You know what is the greatest gift Isobel has ever given me?"

Surprised, I replied, "No, tell me."

"Other than our children," Jared said, "she has given me her forgiveness. I didn't deserve it, but she gave it to me anyway. I just love her so much. I want to be the best husband I can for her."

Just as Jared responded to Isobel's love and forgiveness with a heart that wanted to change, we have a similar opportunity to respond to

God. The apostle Paul tells us, "Don't you realize that the kindness of God leads you to repentance?" (see Romans 2:4). So often we think of repentance as a prerequisite to receiving God's love. We tell ourselves that we need to change *first*, and then we will be accepted and forgiven by God. But the truth is that repentance is a *response to* God's character—his holiness, his love, his kindness, and his grace. Paul tells us that we are saved by grace and not by our efforts to change and "do it right." Salvation is a gift that demonstrates the outrageous kindness of a holy and loving God. There is nothing we can do to earn it. We must simply receive it (Ephesians 2:7-9). However, receiving a gift of such magnitude ought to elicit a response from the depths of our heart.

When I was a child, I loved to watch a particular television program about a benevolent millionaire who gave money to needy people. Each week, a person or family would receive a check in the mail for one million dollars—all they needed to do was cash it. Imagine receiving a call from someone saying you had just been given a million dollars. Such an extravagant gift would call for more than a mere shrug. You would be ecstatic. It would change your life—provided you believed the gift genuine and cashed the check. Jesus speaks of a woman who, after receiving his forgiveness, wet his feet with her tears, kissing them and wiping them with her hair because her heart was filled with love and gratitude for what he had done for her. Her heart responded with love to his gift of love (Luke 7:41-47).

Recently I had the opportunity to watch an Oprah Winfrey show that highlighted random acts of kindness people had done for others. I cried when I saw the people's response to unsolicited acts of kindness on their behalf. It changed them, made them want to do likewise and pass it on. The Bible tells us that the kindness and love of God is meant to change us—to make us want to be more and more like Jesus.

RESPONSES OF THE HEART

Standing in front of the mirror each morning, I face a simple truth. I need a shower, a shampoo, and some makeup before I leave the house. As I face the truth about myself, it propels me into appropriate action. I jump into the shower and begin the process. If I ignored the truth and pretended not to see it, or if I walked out of the house with a bag on my head instead of showering, seeing the truth has not profited me (or anyone else, I might add).

When we are in a relationship with God we are in the very presence of Truth. We cannot stand in his presence and remain neutral. In the final step of the TRUTH Principle, our heart must respond to the truth revealed by God and his Word. We will either bow to God and his truth by changing (repenting), or we will leave his presence and harden our heart.

REBELLION

Patsy brought her seven-year-old daughter, Leah, to see me. Leah was having nightmares and wetting her bed, which had started when the police arrested Leah's dad, a church leader, for fondling Leah and eight other little girls in the church. Patsy was struggling too. How could she have been so blind? Her husband had been accused in previous churches of inappropriate behavior, but he had always denied it. He sounded so convincing. Now the evidence was overwhelming, yet Leah's dad continued to insist that everyone was lying. God was giving him an opportunity to see himself truthfully, for only in that place could he hope to receive the help he needed to make a change. Still, he refused to admit the truth about himself, and he chose to stay deceived and unrepentant. He would not yield his heart to truth or to God. Instead he rebelled, and he exchanged the truth for a lie.

The consequences were tragic. He went to prison, the family broke up (which may have occurred anyway, due to the consequences of his sin), but most tragic of all was that Leah, his little girl, never heard her father say, "Please forgive me. I was so wrong for using you for my own selfish pleasures." Those words may have set into motion young Leah's healing.

Sometimes, even as Christians, we harden our hearts and refuse to yield to God's right to correct and rule us. "O LORD, do not your eyes look for truth? You struck them, but they felt no pain; you crushed them, but they refused correction. They made their faces harder than stone and refused to repent" (Jeremiah 5:3).

For most of us, our rebellion isn't as obvious as Leah's father's. We look good on the outside, but inside our heart is cold, unresponsive to God, and filled with unbelief. Deuteronomy 9:23 says, "But you rebelled against the command of the LORD your God. You did not trust him or obey him." When I got angry with God over the adoption, my heart was filled with unbelief. Although I said I believed *in* God, I didn't *believe* God or his truth enough to walk with him in heartfelt trust and obedience through the pain of my loss. The author of Hebrews tells us that when we have an unbelieving heart, we are rebellious (Hebrews 3:8-19). That is why it is so important for us to take what we learn about God's ways and character and allow it to be transformed from head-based knowledge into heart-based trust.

For others, their entire experience of Christianity could be described as a rule book of dos and don'ts. They always follow the rules, but deep inside, their heart is filled with pride and self-righteousness. They know nothing of the life-giving faith that makes obedience a joy instead of an obligation. Their relationship with God is intellectual, not personal.

Whenever we encounter God, he leaves us with only one of two responses. We will either harden our hearts against him, or we will fall on our face and repent. Many of us would like to repent; however, we often misunderstand what genuine repentance is.

FALSE REPENTANCE: PENANCE

As Christians we often confuse repentance with penance. We see our sin and we're horrified that we're capable of it. This horror comes from the belief that we are basically good people who occasionally do wrong. Our response is to try to do better so we don't feel so badly about ourselves. But penance is man-centered, not God-centered. Penance is an attempt to comfort our wounded pride with the thought that we can do better or can earn God's forgiveness. The truth is that we are sinful people. Why, then, should we be so horrified when we sin?

In chapter 3 we spoke of Debra's struggle with guilt over her hatred toward her mother's dependency on her. She knew it was sinful to allow hateful feelings to fester. So Debra tried harder to be more loving toward her mother. But Debra's efforts came about because she wanted to feel better about herself, not because she asked God to give her a heart to love her mother. This kind of change is deceptive because on the outside it looks right. We love instead of hate; what could be wrong with that? The problem is that we deceive ourselves into believing that we are capable of good in and of ourselves. The result is that we get running on the treadmill of trying harder and harder, believing that this is what God expects and that God will be pleased with us when we achieve it. When we fail, we feel ashamed and weary. Yet God says that there is no good thing in our old natures (Romans 7). He desires us to be entirely dependent upon him for our good. He doesn't expect us to be good apart from his working in us.

Another form of penance takes the form of self-punishment. Such bizarre practices as plucking out one's own beard or striking one's back with a whip made up of small pieces of stone on the tips were not that uncommon several hundred years ago as remedies for sin. While I was in the Philippines, I heard of a practice that occurs during Easter week: Some people are actually nailed to a cross and hang there for the day in public display of remorse for their sin.

We are appalled at these kinds of practices, but here in America we also engage in forms of penance as punishment. One woman I counseled would punch herself in the legs and arms whenever awareness of her sin filled her with self-hatred. Another would stand under the shower with scalding hot water pounding her flesh. Too dramatic? What about withdrawing from friends, dropping out of Bible study, or beating yourself up with words like "I can't believe I could have been so stupid" or "How could I have done such a terrible thing? I'm such a loser." I speak to hundreds of men and women—Christian people— who engage in such practices. They are not able to deal with their sin without such practices of penance.

When we sin, most of us feel guilty and ashamed. That isn't so bad, but it is not enough. Feeling guilty and ashamed about our sin is not the problem. It is what we do with those feelings that is the problem.

TWO KINDS OF SORROW

The apostle Paul speaks of two kinds of sorrow in 2 Corinthians 7. In this passage Paul tells the Corinthians about his anxiousness over a letter he had sent, which rebuked them for wrong living, because he knew it would hurt them. But now, he says, he is glad he sent it, because their sorrow led them to repentance.

Sometimes we think that feeling sorry or regretful is what the Bible means when it speaks of repentance. In 2 Corinthians 7, Paul specifically addresses two kinds of sorrow: One leads to repentance, but the other leads to death. In Matthew 27:3 Judas was "seized with remorse and returned the thirty silver coins to the chief priests and the elders." Judas felt terrible about betraying Christ. He made restitution by returning the silver and even made a confession: "'I have sinned,' he said, 'for I have betrayed innocent blood'" (v. 4). Yet Judas did not repent. Sadly, his response to his sin was to feel so bad he hanged himself.

Sandy came into counseling for depression. She felt like a failure as a mother. "I just can't be what I'm supposed to be," she sobbed after confessing that she had seriously lost her temper with her children. "I could have really hurt them today." Sandy felt guilty and ashamed. She felt sorrow over her sin. However, her sorrow was leading to death, not to experiencing God's forgiveness or to any real change in her parenting. She hated herself because she had failed to live up to her idea of a good mother. Her grief and depression were not related to her sins against God or her children. Her grief stemmed from disappointment in herself. She was not what she thought she was. Her abusive behavior assaulted her pride and self-image, and she could not bear the true picture of who she was.

There is a sorrow over sin that is so deep and a self-hatred so great that the only reasonable course of action to a pride so wounded is self-destruction. This can be achieved through obvious means, like alcohol and drug abuse, promiscuity, or suicide. Or the road to destruction can be more subtle, like striving to be good, wearing masks, and pretending to be what we know we are not. In these ways we fool ourselves into thinking that we are not as bad as we fear we really are. But if Scripture is true when it tells us that the only way to become our true self is through Christ, then any other path will lead to destruction. Even if we look good on the outside, death will eventually occur on the inside.

Fénelon says, "Go forward always with confidence, without letting yourself be touched by the grief of a sensitive pride, which cannot bear to see itself imperfect."[1] The sorrow we feel over our sin can lead us to despair and death, either literally through self-destructive behaviors or emotionally through depression or pretense. God loves us so much that he seeks to separate us from the idolatry of our pride and self-love by giving us a good hard look at the truth of our condition. When we see our sin, sometimes we want to run and hide. We don't want to admit it and come to God, needing his forgiveness. Because of God's great love, he pursues us much as he did Adam and Eve. True repentance is a response of the heart to the holiness of God and to the love and sacrifice of Christ in securing our forgiveness. It causes our heart to respond back with thanksgiving, love, and obedience, which lead to a change of heart and life (see Diagram 6.1).[2]

Genuine repentance involves more than feeling sorry, although that is often the first step. True repentance involves more than our emotions, and more than merely changing our wrong actions or sinful behaviors. It involves the whole heart—our mind, emotions, and will.

True repentance as a "change of mind involves both a turning from sin and a turning to God."[3] First a person does this in his heart, then in his habits. Repentance means agreeing with God and yielding ourselves to his right to rule us. It leads us to make every effort to act accordingly in the daily details of our lives.

Diagram 6.1

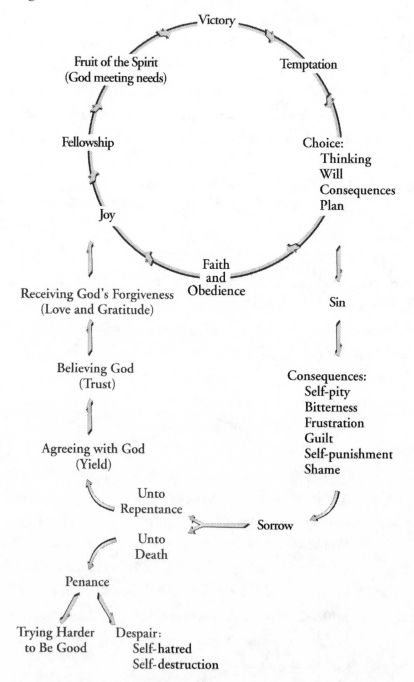

David's prayer of repentance in Psalm 51 is essentially a prayer of agreement with God. David has a broken heart (v. 17), but, more than that, he identifies whom he sinned against and confesses that God is right, just, and true. He agrees with God's judgment of him (v. 4), and asks for cleansing and change (vv. 1,7,10).

THE PROCESS OF REPENTANCE

Repentance for the Christian is an ongoing process, not a once-and-done event. "True repentance is a continued spring, where the waters of godly sorrow are always flowing."[4]

The appropriate response to seeing ourselves truthfully is humility, not self-hatred. "Merely to see how wretched we are and to fall into despair over what we see is not being humble. On the contrary, to do that is to have a fit of pride that cannot consent to being brought low."[5]

When we see ourselves truthfully, we become deeply aware that we are people who need the burning coal of God's cleansing. We cry as Isaiah did, "Woe to me!... I am ruined!" (Isaiah 6:5). "We become disgusted with our evil, and totally dissatisfied with our good."[6]

When we mourn because we have sinned against God we are in the beginning of true repentance. We are sick of our sin. We are sick of ourselves. We are sick of doing things our own way, in our own strength, and we begin to turn. We turn away from our sin. We turn away from ourselves—our solution to life, our version of what we need to make a happy and meaningful life—and we look to Christ, who is our only hope. What we find in him is a loving grace that offers us forgiveness even though we deserve death. We yield to God and receive with needy and open arms what he gives us—his forgiveness and his purpose for our life. Our heart responds with gratitude and love.

This process of self-awareness and repentance in the Christian's life will continue from the day we give our life to Christ until the day we die. We see our true condition and we mourn. This drives us to our knees, to Christ the all-sufficient one, where we can experience his forgiveness and be comforted. Teresa of Avila encourages us to "profit by these faults and learn from them what wretched creatures we are."[7] Our emotions sorrow unto repentance, which leads our mind to confess— to admit our idolatry, sinful thoughts, attitudes, actions, or feelings, and to renounce them. This process disables our inner propensity to make excuses for ourselves or to blame others. In confession we do not apologize; we admit we have sinned and are sinners.[8]

Over the years I have learned a secret that has been tremendously freeing for me in my walk with God. God doesn't expect me to get things right in and of my own efforts. In fact, coming face to face with my own need, being aware of my smallness and my sinful heart, is exactly where God wants me to be. Therefore, he brings me to that place often. It is in this place that I have an opportunity to respond to God by dying to my prideful self and the things that I thought I needed to make life work, giving up my idols, and yielding myself to God and his desire to direct my life. Repentance doesn't stop at brokenness, confession, and renunciation. It continues through the process of yielding our will to God and trusting, preferring, and choosing him to be our very source of life.

GENUINE REPENTANCE ALWAYS INVOLVES CHANGE

Ted and Sara had the garden-variety type of marital issues that bring many couples into counseling. She complained that he didn't listen. He complained that she nagged. They said they loved each other and wanted a good marriage. Week after week, I would give assignments to each of them that would help bring about change, yet nothing happened. Promises were made and broken. Emotions were elevated and apologies profuse, but there were no lasting changes. Their marriage grew more troubled and distant, although both gave lip service to wanting to make it work.

Sin always leads to broken relationships. This occurs in human relationships and it occurs in our relationship with God. When we see our sin but make no effort to change, then how has seeing it profited us or our relationship? Nothing has changed, even if we feel sad or guilty.

Jesus told the Pharisees to produce fruit in keeping with repentance (Matthew 3:8), and the apostle Paul preached to both Jews and Gentiles that they should "repent and turn to God and prove their repentance by their deeds" (Acts 26:20). Repentance is a response of the believer's heart to the voice of God naming sin in her life. Obedience to God's voice is the outgrowth of that repentance. Obedience is not an intellectual acknowledgment of a theological principle or position. That is knowledge, not trust, and keeps Christ at arm's length. Obedience flows from a heart that loves God too much to disappoint him with a wasted life. It comes out of a heart that fears God and doesn't want to take his commands frivolously or lightly. In the last step of the TRUTH Principle, we choose to believe God and yield our heart and life to him and his right to rule us. Jesus tells us that if we love him we will obey him (John 14:23). Love is not mere sentiment. It is both a disposition of our heart and an activity of our mind and will.

Although the Holy Spirit empowers us to change, it is our responsive love for God that motivates us to change. As we grow in faith, we desire to please him more than we desire to please ourselves. When we repent, our desires change. It's not that we don't desire the old things any longer; it's that we have come to love and desire Jesus more.

TIME FOR REFLECTION

1. What is your heart's usual response to the truth of God's Word? Do you respond by choosing to trust and obey him? Or do you just leave it in your head, where it makes very little difference in your heart or life? God calls this unbelief and equates it with rebellion (Hebrews 3:7-19).

2. Do you agree with God's assessment when he reveals to you the things that your heart loves? Have you been willing to repent by confessing and giving those things up (dying to your idols)? Or have your confessions been more like penance—feeling sad and sorrowful but not forsaking your first loves to follow after God?

3. Read Matthew 16:24-26. What part of ourselves must we be willing to "lose" if we are to really find ourselves?

4. What has been your heart's response to the grace and mercy of God in your life? How has his forgiveness changed your heart? Write a psalm or prayer to God for what he has done for you.

PART III

The Pathway to Spiritual Maturity and a Lasting Change of Heart

CHAPTER SEVEN

LIVING TO PLEASE GOD

PRACTICAL APPLICATION OF THE TRUTH PRINCIPLE

If you hold to my teaching, you are really my disciples.
Then you will know the truth, and the truth
will set you free.

JOHN 8:31-32

Many years ago I read an excellent book on discipleship. I was challenged in my walk with the Lord toward greater obedience. I started off strong, but somehow got off track. The problem was not in the book; the problem was in me. I forgot what it said. Sometimes that happens to me after reading the Scriptures or listening to a sermon in church. It is meaningful in the moment, but two days later I'd be hard-pressed to remember exactly what I read or heard. God knows we are forgetful people. That is why in the Scriptures he consistently speaks of creating reminders so that we will not forget him or his ways.

My goal in developing the TRUTH Principle was to make it easy to use and easy to remember, even if it is rigorous to apply. For those who have photographic memories or lots of time for review, there are many wonderful methods for personal growth and discipleship. For the rest of us, however, I hope this model will help you in your journey toward greater Christian maturity as it has helped me in mine.

In the previous chapters, I explained and illustrated each step of the TRUTH Principle. Now it is time to put it all together. One of my colleagues, Sandra Wilson, describes counseling as "private lessons in applied theology."[1] I think that's a good definition. As a counselor I try to guide people toward greater emotional and spiritual maturity using Scripture as our teacher. In this chapter we will begin to explore the ways in which the TRUTH Principle can serve as a guide—a road map, so to speak—to maturity and godliness. The TRUTH Principle can help us understand more clearly where we currently stand in the process; it can also show us where we need to go.

A REVIEW: USING TRUTH FOR PERSONAL GROWTH AND DISCIPLESHIP

T = TROUBLE (CHAPTER 2)

The first step is to identify your trouble. What problem(s) are you facing right now? It might be a big trouble, such as a serious health crisis, marital distress, or job loss. Or you might be dealing with the more common troubles that you encounter throughout the day.

If we are to grow, we need to look at our troubles in a different way than we have in the past, even if the trouble causes us considerable pain. As we mature in our Christian faith, we need to look at troubles through the lens of God's eternal purposes and try to identify what God is up to in our life. How did Jesus or his disciples view troubles and hardships? In order to become more like Christ, we need to learn to look at troubles in the same way he did.

Alice and David are a young couple who had four great kids. One morning, Sammy, their youngest, woke up with a headache. Alice gave him some medication and kept him home from school. Later she noticed he had a slight fever and called the doctor. "Nothing to worry about," he told her. "The flu is going around." Early that evening Sammy started convulsing. They rushed him to the hospital, where he lapsed into a coma and died. The autopsy was inconclusive. "An over-whelming infection hit his organs, and they shut down." This was the only explanation they got. Alice and David were beset with grief and confusion.

If you have experienced this kind of life-changing trouble, Bible verses about God's sovereignty, love, and purposes probably feel flat and lifeless. Often they enrage rather than comfort.

"If God is so loving, then why did he allow this to happen?" we cry. Our heart is hurt and angry that we have been thrust into some unbearable circumstance of life. Job felt this way; so did Jeremiah. They expressed their honest emotions before the Lord. During our troubles, we need not worry that our strong emotions anger God. Even Jesus cried out, "My God, my God, why have you forsaken me?" (Matthew 27:46). God uses our troubles to bring us into a deeper awareness of his nature. Discovering it is part of our maturity. Our faith changes from head knowledge to living, dynamic trust.

R = RESPONSE (CHAPTER 3)

The second step of the TRUTH Principle is looking at our response, or self-examination. We need to understand how we think, feel, and behave in response to our troubles. Some of us need to spend extra time in this step because we have not learned to take personal respon-sibility for our thoughts, our feelings, and our actions. Instead it has been our habit to blame others or to rationalize or to make excuses.

Sometimes we can start the process by identifying our feelings first.

They usually act like warning bells that something is wrong. We can then backtrack and see what situation or trouble elicited those feelings, and what thoughts and behaviors we experienced as a result.

I was in a hurry, anxious to get to the quiet retreat where I had planned to write. I only had five precious days, and I didn't want to waste a moment. To save time, I decided to get some groceries before I left so I wouldn't have to look for a store once I reached my destination. The store wasn't crowded. I quickly got my few items and then rushed to the express checkout line.

In front of me was a woman with four items. Each one was a different type of organic vegetable. The checker was new and didn't know how to locate the price of these things. He was cautious and slow. As the minutes ticked away I could feel my heart beating faster and faster. My breathing turned into muffled snorts as I tried (in a not-so-subtle way) to signal that I was in a hurry! My feelings let me (and others around me) know there was a problem. Was my problem the trouble with the checkout clerk? Not really. He just brought it out. The problem was in me! God was trying to teach me, as he had many times before, to be patient. It's been a struggle. He uses these little troubles in life to give me plenty of practice sessions. Sometimes I recognize them and cooperate; many times I don't.

God will often use the troubles in our lives to give us opportunities to practice the very responses that he wants us to develop—the character of Christ within. By being mindful of these opportunities we can cooperate with the Holy Spirit as we learn the ways of Christ.

U = UNDERLYING IDOLS (CHAPTER 4)

If we really want to follow Christ, we can't stop at knowing the truth; Christ wants more. He wants us to love him with everything we have—all our heart, all our mind, and all our strength. Too often we commit spiritual adultery by letting other loves rule our heart instead of our love for God and his love for us. In identifying the idols of our heart we need to ask, "What do I want?" Another question might be, "What do I love or fear more than God right now?"

I am a married woman. Certain unspoken rules accompany the concept of marriage, such as "married women don't flirt with men who aren't their husband." I don't follow that rule because it's a rule. I don't flirt with other men because I love my husband and don't want to hurt him. I didn't get married because someone told me to, nor because it was the right thing to do. I got married because I chose to. I loved him and desired to be his wife. He and I are in an intimate relationship. When we argue, or when I'm selfish or impatient, our relationship suffers, perhaps because in those moments I love myself more than I love my husband.

Throughout the Scriptures, God uses marriage as a metaphor for his relationship with us. In Hosea 2:19-20 God says "I will betroth you to myself for ever, betroth you in lawful wedlock with unfailing devotion and love; I will betroth you to myself to have and to hold, and you shall know the LORD" (NEB).

Just as my husband would be jealous, angry, and hurt if I started loving other men, God experiences these emotions when we allow our heart to be drawn to other loves. If our relationship with God matters to us, we will be careful to guard our heart and its affections so that nothing separates us from our fellowship with God.

The only thing we have to give back to God for all he has done for us is our love, exercised through our free will. Jesus always wanted what God wanted. Their relationship was one of perfect union. That is to be our goal as we mature. By asking, "What do I want right now?" and contrasting the answer with what God wants, we expose our idols. Then we can yield ourselves to God's right to rule us, just as Jesus did when he said in Gethsemane, "If it is possible, may this cup be taken from me. Yet not as I will, but as you will" (Matthew 26:39). Or, like Eve, we can take matters into our own hands and push forward to get what we want.

Sometimes we get confused and convince ourselves that God endorses what we want; therefore we're entitled to it. We believe God wants us to be happy or to have a good marriage or to be on time or to enjoy any number of things. Believing this makes us push all the harder to get our way. It's not that God doesn't want us to have those things. But when circumstances prevent us from attaining them, we must yield to God and believe that he may have something different in mind.

T = TRUTH (CHAPTER 5)

If we come to understand ourselves more fully but then fail to put ourselves under the light of God's truth, we will never come into spiritual maturity. As we enter this step of the TRUTH Principle, we need to ask, "What is the truth about my trouble—not as I see it, but as God sees it?" Other questions to ask include "What is the truth about how I'm responding to my trouble?" "Who is God to me right now?" "How does that compare to how he describes himself?" and "Do I believe and trust him, or do I trust myself?"

Several years ago I got the itch to redecorate my kitchen. I found some green-checked wallpaper on sale and bought it. I had never wallpapered before, but because I like challenges, I read up on it and decided I could save money by doing it myself. Everything went smoothly until I got to the doorway. It was only then that I realized my paper was crooked. To my eye it had *looked* straight. But when the paper had to line up with the doorway, the checks veered to the left. I had to rip it all off and start over, beginning this time with a plumb line.

The book of 2 Timothy warns us about straying from the truth. God's Word is our plumb line for life. Timothy cautions us not to become like those who are "always learning but never able to acknowledge the truth" (2 Timothy 3:7). The world has lost its sense of objective truth. Truth has become relative, subject to anyone's ability to accept it as true. As Christians we need to be submissive to a higher authority, who is Truth. Truth is not in us; it is in him. It *is* him! We access truth as we yield ourselves and allow the Spirit of God to teach us.

H = HEART'S RESPONSE (CHAPTER 6)

Someone once said, "Insight is the booby prize of life." Seeing the truth won't profit us if it does not change us. In the book of Nehemiah, we find the Israelites far from God. When Nehemiah began instructing them from the Scriptures and making it clear to them who God is and what he required of them, they began a process of repentance and change (Nehemiah 7 and 8).

The final step in the TRUTH Principle is to ask "What is my heart's response to the truth of God's love? To the kindness of God's grace? To the reality of the cross? Do I ignore it? Do I feel bad about myself or my sin and wallow in self-hatred or self-pity? Or do I truly repent?" As God helps us relocate our faith from our head to our heart, he does not kill our desires. Instead, he transforms them and leads us to obedience. Obedience is not conformity to an external standard of belief. Obedience means yielding our will to God's. This can only occur in our heart, where it then affects our outward actions, attitudes, and disposition.

EXERCISING THE TRUTH PRINCIPLE IN THE DAY-TO-DAY TROUBLES OF LIFE

I am sitting in a terrible traffic jam. I am supposed to be at a seminar shortly, and I know I will never make it on time. My heart is racing, my palms are sweating, my temperature is rising, and I am tempted to honk my horn and yell out the window. As I stew about my *trouble* (sitting in traffic), I start to work my way through the TRUTH Principle. What is my *response* to my trouble? I'm feeling angry, anxious, and impatient. I am telling myself that this is awful, that I hate sitting in traffic, and that I should have left earlier. Are there any *underlying idols* in this situation? In order to find out, I need to ask myself some questions. First, what do I want right now? I want to be on time. I want to be out of this traffic! I want things to go smoothly, and I don't want to wait! Next, I need to ask myself what do I love and/or fear the most in this moment? I love a hassle-free life. I fear the embarrassment of walking in late and having to make excuses as to why I'm late for the seminar. What is the idol? Generally I find that it is not *what* I desire but the fact that I desire it too much.

What is the *truth*? How does God see my trouble? I remind myself that God is in control. He has ordered my day. I cannot change anything in this situation except my response to my trouble. In this moment, I can either trust him by yielding to him what my heart wants (to be on time, to save face, and to have a hassle-free life), or I can try harder to make life work on my own. Which will it be? In this situation, my *heart's response* is to yield to God, sit patiently, and wait for the traffic to start moving again. I don't know the why—and I have learned over the years that I don't need to. That is part of trust. And the wonderful result is that by working myself through the steps of the TRUTH

Principle, the anxiety and anger that plagued me moments earlier no longer rule me. I still don't enjoy sitting in traffic jams or being late for meetings, but I can bear the events in a way that pleases God.

CAROL'S OFFENSE

Just as I applied the TRUTH Principle when I found myself aggravated sitting in a traffic jam, I can use the model in any situation I encounter throughout my day. My friend Carol described to me how she used the TRUTH Principle when she found out that her daughter didn't make her high-school varsity basketball team. Carol felt upset and hurt, both for herself and for her daughter. She was angry at the coach who cut her daughter from the team and felt that the selection process was unfair. She was anxious that her daughter would take it hard and perhaps get involved in less constructive pursuits in high school. She was tempted to march into the coach's office and give him a piece of her mind.

Instead, Carol worked herself through this situation using the TRUTH Principle. First, she asked herself what her trouble was. She put it down on paper so she could get a good look at it.

My trouble: My daughter got cut from the team.

Next, Carol looked at her response to her troubles. Charting your responses on paper can be a helpful way to examine your thoughts, feelings, and behaviors more carefully. Taking this step is important in understanding yourself better. Just like Carol, as you work through the TRUTH Principle with your particular trouble, you may want to make a written chart. When you become more familiar with this step, you can do it mentally. (See Chart 7.1 on page 146.)

Chart 7.1

Trouble	Thoughts	Feelings	Behavior
My daughter got cut from the team.	She didn't deserve this.	anger	
	The coach was unfair.	anger	
	What if she takes this really hard?	anxiousness	
	I can't believe this happened to her.	sadness	
	Why did this happen to her?	sadness	
	The coach was unfair.	anger	
	He should be fired.	anger	
	He doesn't know what he's doing.	anger	
	He plays favorites.	anger	
	What if she gets involved with the wrong kids now?	anxiousness	
	I can't bear to see her hurting.	sadness, pain	

Since Carol hadn't taken any action yet, she left the behavior column of her chart blank.

The chart gave Carol a much clearer understanding of her feelings and *why* she was feeling them. She could see how her feelings were triggered—not by the trouble, but by the specific thoughts she was having *about* her trouble.

Next, Carol wanted to see if she had any idols in her heart. Was there more to this incident than what she had uncovered thus far? Carol began to ask herself questions to uncover the desires of her heart. What did she want in this moment? What did she love? What did she fear? This was difficult for Carol. She wasn't used to thinking about what she wanted. She sometimes felt guilty when she acknowledged, even to herself, what she really wanted. This is what Carol came up with.

1. I wanted my daughter to make the team.

2. I want my daughter to be happy.

3. I want my daughter to be treated fairly.

4. I want my daughter to be a good athlete.

5. I love watching my daughter play basketball.

6. I love feeling like a good mom, and I feel like a good mom when my daughter is involved in good things like sports.

7. I fear how my daughter will respond to this disappointment.

8. I fear what people will think of me if she responds poorly.

The reason it is important for Carol to admit to and look at the desires of her heart is that our desires rule us (see chapter 4). For Christians, most of the time our desires are not blatantly sinful desires. They are usually good and legitimate desires that have become too important and that get in the way of God's best for us. What happened to Carol when she didn't get what she wanted?

The next step Carol implemented was to look at her trouble from God's perspective (Truth). As Carol spent time with God in prayer, she began to see her troubles differently. (Remember, prayer doesn't always change our situation, but prayer often changes the way we look at it.) She began to talk honestly with God about the desires of her heart and her feelings about not having those desires met. In that process God reminded Carol that he loves her daughter more than she possibly could, and that she would need to trust him to bring good out of this situation. He also reminded her of several psalms, such as Psalms 55 and 73, that recalled times when David was treated unfairly. God both knew and understood.

God also began to gently point out to Carol that she was too dependent on her image as a good mom. She would need to learn not to fear others' criticisms of her mothering if she was ever to be free to be a truly good mother.

Carol responded to God's truth by choosing to believe him, and trusting him to know what was best for her daughter. Once she made that choice, she found herself emotionally able to handle her legitimate disappointment in a way that honored God. She was also then ready to begin moving her heart toward forgiving the coach, whom she still believed was unfair and played favorites. But instead of just reacting and marching into his office to give him a piece of her mind, she considered it and prayed about whether it would be helpful to the coach and to her daughter to speak to him about his methods of selecting the team. Most important, Carol was empowered to *be* a good mother and help her daughter move through this disappointment in a mature way.

Sometimes we think that taking the time to work our way through the minor events in our life is unimportant to our overall maturity. However, it is in the faithful practice of working through these steps in the little things that we grow in strength and perseverance to handle the bigger problems of life.

PHILIP'S JOB LOSS

At fifty-two years old, Philip never imagined that he would be laid off from the company where he had worked for twenty five years. He was devastated. He was tempted to become overwhelmed with fear and to give in to depression. The TRUTH Principle gave Philip a tool to use to help himself through his difficulty.

Philip's obvious trouble was his job loss. What was his response to his trouble? (See Chart 7.2.)

We can easily see that some of Philip's thoughts were rational; others were not. One thing Philip needed to do was challenge his irrational thoughts with the truth. His internal dialogue, which insisted he was a failure and he would never be able to get through this, disabled him.

Chart 7.2

Trouble	Thoughts	Feelings	Behaviors
job loss	I can't believe this happened.	shock	withdrew from family and friends
	What am I going to do?	anxiousness	moped around the house
	What if I don't find another job?	fear	
	How am I going to survive?	fear	
	Who's going to hire a fifty-two-year-old man?	depression	slept a lot
	I'm just a failure.	depression	
	I'll never be able to get through this.	hopelessness	

After working steadily for the same company for over twenty-five years, his conclusion that he was a failure certainly was not true.

Looking deeper helped Philip understand himself more fully. What were the possible underlying idols in his heart? What did he want? Philip wanted to work. He wanted to have his old job back. He wanted to have a steady income to support himself and his family. He loved the security of knowing that his bills were going to be paid and that he was saving for his retirement. He feared the loss of his savings, his home, and his self-esteem. He feared that being laid off would impact his future employment prospects and that others would think less of him.

The desires of Philip's heart are normal desires that, to some degree, we all have. Feeling uncertain and scared when faced with the loss of something dear to us is a common human response. That is why the next step in the TRUTH Principle is so crucial to our well-being. During this kind of trouble we all face the question, "Does the reality of our relationship with God meet us in our deepest need?" Do we really trust God? Does his truth speak to our innermost heart? Does it have the power to calm the unrest and turmoil that is stirring within and help us face life in a courageous way?

As Philip spent time pouring his heart out to God and his Christian friends, he found himself reminded of what is true: God had not abandoned him. He knew Philip's situation and was in control of it. He would provide. Through the support of God's Word and God's people, these promises became deeper realities for Philip and his family as they walked through the trouble of his job loss. Although he desired the same things as he did earlier, these desires did not rule his heart. He wanted what God wanted more than he wanted his old job back, more than he wanted financial security.

Philip's heart could have responded in anger or unbelief. These are temptations that we all face when we lose control and don't know what is going to happen next. Yet God always seeks to deepen our dependence on him and our trust in him. Often he uses the troubles in our life to accomplish that very purpose.

Jesus said, "You will know the truth, and the truth will set you free" (John 8:32). Free from the old nature's ways and habits. Free to shed all that is contrary to his likeness in us. Free to become all he wants us to be. Free to become our true self in Christ. Paul tells us in Ephesians 4:22-24: "You were taught, with regard to your former way of life, to put off your old self, which is being corrupted by its *deceitful desires*; to be made new in the attitude of your minds; and to put on the *new self, created to be like God in true righteousness and holiness*" (italics mine).

TIME FOR REFLECTION

1. Begin to memorize the steps in the TRUTH Principle. In a journal, identify a particular trouble you are facing and then answer the questions below:

T. What is the *trouble* I'm facing? What could God be up to in my trouble?

R. How have I *responded* to my trouble? What do I think and feel? Have I noticed how my thoughts influence my feelings? How am I behaving in the midst of my trouble?

U. What are the *underlying idols* in my heart? What do I want right now? What do I love or fear the most? What is ruling me?

T   .

What is the *truth?* Who is God to me, and what is his perspective? Do I believe and trust him?

H. What is my *heart's response* to God? Have I repented of the idols in my heart? Have I embraced the things he has shown me and practiced them in the daily habits of my life?

When you find yourself troubled or feeling upset, begin to apply the steps of the TRUTH principle to your situation. Notice where you get stuck. Perhaps these are areas in which God desires you to mature. What could you begin doing to trust him more? How could you practice applying his truth to the troubles in your life?

2. Each day practice walking yourself through the steps of the TRUTH Principle when you find yourself in some minor difficulties. Notice what difference it makes in how you handle the situation and the effect it has on your emotions as you go through the process. As you gain maturity in handling small difficulties, you will find yourself better prepared to handle more serious troubles that God may allow in your life.

CHAPTER EIGHT

THE BIG PICTURE

USING THE TRUTH PRINCIPLE TO REVEAL
IDOLATROUS LIFE THEMES

We instructed you how to live in order to please God....
Now we ask you and urge you in the Lord Jesus
to do this more and more.

1 THESSALONIANS 4:1

There are many good books that describe what needs to change in our life and what a mature Christian is supposed to look like. But they often don't show *how* to get from point A to point B. As we discussed in chapter 7, the TRUTH Principle can be that road map. It can be used to talk yourself through a minor irritant of life, like a traffic jam, and it can help you navigate a much more life-altering trouble, like a divorce or a major illness. As you gain experience in working with the TRUTH Principle, you may want to expand your application of it: Not only can it assist you in the troubles of life, but it can also help you achieve deeper personal change in pervasive habits.

Gina came into counseling with clinical depression and low self-esteem. In her words, her life was "a mess." Gina was in debt, the result of poor spending habits. She found it difficult to use her time wisely and never seemed to have time for regular devotions or exercise. Her health was deteriorating, but when the doctor recommended a special diet, Gina found it impossible to maintain. "I just can't seem to do it," she cried. "It's too hard." Gina's relationships were superficial, and she avoided going out with her friends. "I'm just too depressed," she said.

What were Gina's troubles? Specifically, they were her money problems, her health problems, her time-management problems, and her relationship problems. As we look at Gina's response to her troubles, we see that she felt overwhelmed and depressed. She told herself change was too difficult and she was too weak. She told herself it wasn't fair that God allowed her life to be so hard. Gina indulged herself for comfort. She shopped, watched television, or ate too much as a way of coping with her difficult and unsatisfying life.

Now any one of these areas would give a counselor plenty of things to work on. Should I help Gina to feel better about herself so she won't be so depressed and will perhaps be empowered to tackle some of her problems? Should I help her to learn time-management techniques and money-management skills so she can control her impulse spending? Should I explore Gina's family background and personal history to see if abuse or addiction problems have influenced her current situation? Any of these strategies might be appropriate and even necessary at the proper time, but not yet. First, I needed to help Gina expose her heart so that lasting change could take place.

What were her underlying idols? What ruled Gina's heart? Gina was a Christian. She went to church regularly. Gina said she loved God, but she also had other loves. What did she want? When we talked, I discovered Gina loved pleasure, fun, and a good time. She wanted relief and a pain-free life. Gina saw God more or less as a "psychic errand boy"[1] who was supposed to come through to give her a great life. In her mind, he existed to serve her and make her happy.

From Gina's perspective, he wasn't doing such a good job.

As we began to look at Gina's troubles in light of the truth, I began to challenge her with the thought that God might be using her difficulties to develop something *in* her. A verse that was especially helpful to Gina was Proverbs 15:32: "He who ignores discipline despises himself." Could it be that Gina's depression and low self-esteem were the result of inadequate self-discipline to deal with her problems maturely rather than the result of her troubles themselves? Could it be that God, in his faithful love for Gina, was working in her to develop the very discipline that would help her to mature and, ultimately, to feel more positive about herself?

As Gina took time to absorb what God was teaching her, her heart began to respond in faith to God. Her picture of him changed from that of an errand boy who served her into that of a loving Father who disciplined her so she would not continue to hurt herself. He wanted her to grow up and serve him. Her heart began to repent of the sinful, self-destructive ways in which she thought, acted, and lived. She also began to recognize that she loved pleasure more than God. As an outgrowth of her repentance, Gina began to take small steps of self-discipline that would help her to stop her old patterns and develop new ones. As she began to practice these steps and develop self-control, something happened in Gina. She began to feel better about herself, and her depression lifted.

DIGGING DEEPER

Like Gina, as you become more familiar with using the TRUTH Principle in your daily life, you may notice repeated themes that emerge both in your responses to your troubles and in the idols of your heart. The TRUTH Principle can be used to help us work on long-standing character or personality weaknesses that dominate many of our day-to-day struggles. Our temperament influences the way we work, think, and interact with our families and friends. In our journey toward Christlike character, God seeks to bring balance and maturity to our life through the power of his Spirit, who lives and works within our heart. Our areas of weakness are often difficult to see, let alone change. Often it helps if we can work with other Christians who are more mature than we are and who can help us see the truth about ourselves and our situation more clearly.

JACK—THE CONTROLLER

Remember Jack, from chapters 3 and 4? Jack regularly lost his temper with his wife, Mary. As a Christian, Jack acknowledged that his angry temper was sinful and that it hurt his relationship with Mary. Yet, after years of trying, he still could not get a consistent handle on his outbursts of anger. How could Jack better understand himself, and what should he do in order to be able to be more consistent in managing his temper?

What was Jack's trouble? Basically, Jack became troubled over anything that he didn't like or anything that didn't go the way he thought it should. Often he experienced this in his relationship with his wife, but there were also other areas of life that caused Jack trouble. For example, when his subordinates at work made mistakes or didn't complete their tasks as he would have liked, Jack became critical. When his children misbehaved or were careless or foolish, Jack often blew up.

In using the TRUTH Principle to understand Jack's trouble, we could approach it incident by incident, as we did in chapter 3, where Jack's trouble was the fact that Mary failed to put the pens and pencils back in the drawer. Or we could take a much larger look at Jack's trouble and describe it as whenever things did not go his way.

The next step of the TRUTH Principle is for Jack to understand more fully his general response to his troubles. Initially Jack blamed Mary for his outbursts of anger. He did not understand that his responses were coming out of his own heart. He believed that if only Mary wouldn't do the things that upset him, he would not feel the way he did. This kind of thinking is subtly deceptive because there is an ounce of truth to it. Obviously, if Mary had put the pens and pencils back in the drawer, Jack wouldn't have gotten angry—this time. However, the basic theme of Jack's life—"Things should always go the way I want them to go"—would be left unexamined.

Working through the *R* step of the TRUTH Principle helps us identify first our feelings and then the thoughts that contribute to those feelings, instead of blaming the troubles that brought those feelings to the surface. As you take the time to do this, you will notice that certain themes repeat themselves. For example, when Jack examined his thoughts after various incidents, four themes emerged:

1. Things should always go the way I want them to go.

2. Other people should think of me and do what I want.

3. People should notice me and respect my wants and feelings.

4. People should stop doing things that upset me.

Jack had lots of "shoulds" for other people to live by. Their failure to live up to his expectations triggered his angry responses.

To go deeper yet is to look for the broader underlying idols of the heart. The *U* step in the TRUTH Principle is crucial, because Jack won't permanently change by just learning to control his temper or by having better responses to his troubles. So often that is where we get on the treadmill of trying harder and harder, only to find ourselves eventually failing. If Jack doesn't look at the idols that rule his heart, he will respond the same way over and over again, even if he tries not to. By examining what he loved or wanted the most, Jack was able to see more clearly what ruled his heart.

Again, the TRUTH Principle can be used to get a snapshot perspective (in other words, "What do I want in this moment?"), or it can be used in a broader way to search for the idols that regularly rule our heart.

For Jack, the ruling idol of his heart was wanting to have things go his way. He wanted everyone to think of his needs first, and he *used* his anger to exert power and control over the people in his life to ensure that would happen. If Jack changed his behavior by learning anger-management techniques, ultimately he would have used more socially acceptable means of getting his own way. But the core problem of Jack's selfishness and his idol of power and control would never have been addressed or changed.

These deeply held beliefs can sometimes be very difficult to see without outside help. The heart is deceitful, and we don't tend to challenge what we want.

As we expose the idols of our heart, it is important to challenge them with the truth of God's Word. In this step of the TRUTH Principle, Jack had to ask himself, "Is it true that everything should go the way I want or expect? Is it true that others should always cater to what I want first?" Jack got stuck on this step because he believed it *was* true—especially with Mary and his children. He believed that God *wanted* him to have what he wanted—like love, submission, understanding, order, and obedience; therefore, he could not see how these were wrong. "As a Christian husband I have a right to these things," he would say. He also believed that as the head of his house, he had the authority to punish those who did not comply. As long as Jack believed these things, his anger continued to serve his ruling idol through his use of power and control to get what he wanted. It would be very hard for him to give it up.

Eventually, much of Jack's growth and maturity came from his willingness to allow other Christians to show him the truth about God. Jack needed to see God in a different light. In the *truth* step of our model, Jack needed to see he wasn't looking at himself or his situation from God's perspective. He was using God to meet his agenda. Scriptures that spoke of servanthood, forbearance, patience, and loving others were only words on a page to Jack. They had no meaning or purpose in his life. The verses that Jack loved and used were ones that served his idol. He used the Scriptures to control and manipulate others in much the same way as he used his anger. In order for Jack to have a change of heart, he needed to allow the truth of God's Word to speak to him. Jack needed to see how God responds when we don't do what he wants. Jack needed to see how Jesus treated people who disappointed him. Jack needed to learn much more about mercy, grace, and love.

Many of us sit in church week after week listening to good teaching, but our heart wants what it wants and therefore does not respond to God's truth with submission and repentance. Instead, we try to figure out how to feel better, get our way, or justify our own agenda. Initially this was Jack's response. However, a part of Jack really did want to be different and to grow up in Christ. It was in this part of Jack that the truth of God's Word took root. As he worked to comprehend the reality of God's grace and love, his heart began to soften.

Merely knowing about truth won't change us. Only as we respond with our heart in trust and obedience to the truth do we begin to change. This is the final step in the TRUTH Principle. Jack's heart began to respond to God's love and grace toward him. His heart wanted to love back. He started to understand that love gives; it doesn't demand its own way (1 Corinthians 13). Rather than simply being sorry for losing his temper, Jack learned to repent of his demand to have everything go his way. He started to catch himself when he found himself getting angry. Instead of learning to control his temper, he began to yield to God his desire to have his own way and to have everyone cater to him. As he did that, he found that things did not upset him quite as easily as they used to. He still desired Mary's love, her understanding, her submission, and order in the home. But now he was willing to let her give them to him rather than demand them from her. When she failed him, he learned to forgive instead of to punish her.

In the process, Jack had to yield his desire for power and control to God, who truly *is* in control. Jack wrestled with a universal question: Does God know what he is doing when he doesn't give me my heart's desires? As Jack learned to trust God more, he could let go of control in his relationships and observe and understand how God used these relationships to develop the fruit of the Spirit in his heart—like patience, kindness, self-control, and love.

These changes took time. It didn't happen in six weeks or even in six months. At times Mary wasn't sure she could or would hang in there. Jack had to allow the larger body of Christ to minister to him. He needed to read God's Word with an open heart and not just to prove his points. Jack had to learn to practice patience and forbearance in the little things, which prepared him to better handle bigger disappointments. He had to learn how to forgive and let go of hurts and disappointments. He had to learn to live for Christ and not for himself.

As Jack committed himself to this process, he began to mature—spiritually and emotionally.

MARY—THE PLEASER

Mary had a very different approach to life than Jack did. She hated conflict and avoided it whenever she could. That worked great for Jack, because it meant he usually got his way. If Jack raised his voice, Mary would cringe. Mary usually tried hard to please Jack so she could avoid unpleasant scenes. However, her natural lack of organization continued to be a source of conflict between them. Although she tried, inevitably she would somehow fail to meet Jack's expectations.

Mary described her trouble as her tumultuous relationship with her husband. Let's look at Mary's responses to her trouble (see Chart 8.1).

Over the period of time that I knew Mary, it became obvious that

Chart 8.1

Trouble	Thoughts	Feelings	Behaviors
Jack is mad!	Oh no, here we go again!	anxiousness	withdraw
	Why didn't I just remember what he wanted?	anger toward self	try harder to please Jack
	I can't stand it when he's mad at me.	depression	cry
	What if he leaves me?	fear	cry
	Why can't he stop yelling at me?	hurt	cry

her feelings and behaviors represented repeated themes in her relationships, not only with her husband, but also with her mother, her younger sister, and some church friends. Once, one of Mary's friends dropped off three baskets of laundry for Mary to wash and iron. Her friend reasoned since she worked full-time and Mary was at home "with nothing to do," Mary could surely help her by doing her laundry. Mary never said no, and it quickly became a weekly chore. Mary was a pleaser and a peacekeeper, which meant never saying no or setting boundaries. Whatever Mary had to do to avoid conflict, she would do.

Let's look at the underlying idols of Mary's heart. They were very different from Jack's. When I asked Mary about the desires of her heart, she said, "I just want a good marriage. I want to be happy, and I want Jack to be happy with me. I want people to appreciate all I try to do for them. I want people to like me and to be happy with me. I want to have a peaceful home life. And I don't want to ever make anyone upset with me."

What did Mary love? She loved serenity and peace. She loved things to go smoothly with no bumps in the road. She loved pleasing others, and she loved it when people were happy with her. She became fearful when others were displeased. She believed that she was somehow responsible for their anger or disappointment with her. She feared people would end their relationship with her if she didn't make them happy. She feared that if she told them how she really felt, they would become angry with her.

The next step for Mary is to look at the truth. What does God have to say to Mary about her "manner of life"? For one thing, Proverbs 29:25 says, "Fear of man will prove to be a snare." Mary's heart was ruled by the fear of man. She loved people's approval and feared their disapproval. Most of us can relate to the desire for people to like us, but that desire ruled Mary's life. She did whatever it took to make sure people liked her, even if it meant compromising her own feelings or well-being. When she feared she wasn't getting what her heart craved, she became filled with anxiety.

As I worked with Mary on these things, I found out that she believed God wanted her to please people and to always think of other people's needs first. She had always been taught that it was selfish to think of herself or to say no unless she absolutely could not do something—and she'd better have a very, very good reason. Mary needed to understand that she was not "loving others" when she met their needs out of fear. In fact, if she wanted to move toward loving her husband in a God-centered way, she would need to risk rejection. Instead of withdrawing from Jack during a marital conflict, she would need to develop the courage to speak the truth in love to him about his destructive attitudes and actions. Mary needed to find her security and well-being in her relationship with Jesus rather than in her relationship with others. Only then would she be strong enough to do the things she needed to do without being crippled by fear.

As Mary's heart grasped the truth of what God was showing her, she began to see in the Scriptures that at times people weren't pleased with Jesus. He was perfect, yet people didn't always agree with what he did. At times he said no, and at other times he spoke the truth to people who weren't receptive to his words. Mary responded to this revelation by agreeing with God that her desires and fears ruled her heart. She agreed she would need to lessen the importance of people's opinions of her if she ever was going to be free to be all God had designed her to be.

Mary began to risk conflict in small ways by starting to say no to people. First she practiced on strangers. Then she moved on to saying no to people whose opinions mattered most to her. She found that sometimes people did get angry with her. When she finally told her friend that she could no longer do her laundry, her friend was disappointed and mildly angry. Yet Mary stayed firm and said that she valued their friendship too much to let herself continue to feel taken advantage of. She needed to speak up. She hoped her friend would accept her feelings. The biggest change in Mary came when she didn't *need* her friend to understand or accept her feelings. It would have been nice if she did, but it wouldn't cripple Mary if her friend didn't accept them.

As Mary worked herself through the steps of the TRUTH Principle, she began to strengthen her relationship with God. As Mary learned to believe God more and experience his unconditional love and acceptance of her, she could let go of her cravings for the approval and acceptance of others. She began to see how God used those opportunities to develop more godly characteristics in her, characteristics like boldness and the ability to speak the truth in love. By setting boundaries so that she would not be ruled by the whims and agendas of other people, she started to become a God-pleaser, not a people-pleaser. As Mary deepened her love relationship with Jesus, she began to learn what it means to live for Christ and not for others.

The following charts help us locate some of the underlying idols of our heart as well as the negative personality traits that may accompany those idols. God's desire always is to move our heart away from anything that hinders our relationship with him and that hampers our ability to become more like him. If we are to grow into our fullest maturity, just changing our behaviors will never be enough. Our idolatrous desires will need to be yielded to God, so that nothing we desire compares with him (Psalm 73:25). (See Charts 8.2 and 8.3.)

Chart 8.2

DESIRES OF OUR HEART

What do I love?	Possible negative personality traits	Sinful behavioral and emotional tendencies
pleasure	indulgent, selfish, self-centered	substance abuser, overeater, overspender, gambler, party person, lazy, procrastinator
power	controller	outburst of anger, critical, argumentative, bossy, authoritative, insensitive to others' feelings
peace (hates conflict)	avoider/pretender	passive, dishonest, withdraws from conflict, never resolves problems
praise/approval	pleaser/pretender	fears rejection, seeks recognition and love, codependent
perfection	striver	overachiever, workaholic, critical, anxious or depressed (because nothing is ever good enough in self or others)

Chart 8.3

FEARS OF OUR HEART

What do I fear?	Possible negative personality traits	Sinful behavioral and emotional tendencies
failure	quitter, overachiever, striver	quitter, procrastinator, despondent, driven to succeed, workaholic
rejection	pleaser	codependent, compliant, dishonest with feelings, dependent
humiliation	controller	angry, intimidating manner, superior attitude
conflict	peacekeeper	avoider, hider, wears masks, pretender
intimacy	withdrawer	aloof, cold, withdrawn, avoider

JESUS AS OUR EXAMPLE OF FULL MATURITY

In Matthew 26, we can read the familiar story of Jesus in the Garden of Gethsemane. What was the trouble? Jesus was facing his own death. What was his response to his trouble? He said, "My soul is overwhelmed with sorrow to the point of death" (v. 38). Jesus never sugarcoated his feelings. He felt as we would in this situation. He knows, therefore, how we feel when we are faced with troubles and difficult situations (Hebrews 4:15). Sometimes we think that becoming a mature Christian means we will never experience the more negative emotions in response to our troubles. We think that somehow we should face all our troubles feeling happy with a song in our heart. This is simply not true. Jesus experienced deep sorrow and anguish in the midst of his troubles.

What did Jesus want? What were the desires of his heart? The account says he wanted two things. First, he wanted his friends, his disciples, to pray for him. Second, he wanted the cup of death to be taken from him. Isn't that often what we want? We want the people who care about us to meet our needs, and we want to be rid of our troubles. Yet Jesus willingly yielded those desires to God's plan. Jesus lived his life to please the Father, not himself. He said, "My Father, if it is not possible for this cup to be taken away unless I drink it, may your will be done" (Matthew 26:42). Jesus fully yielded his heart to God. He was responsive and submissive to God's plan. His friends disappointed him. God didn't take away his trouble, and Jesus went willingly to the cross. He is our example to follow. We are to become like him. The author of Hebrews encourages us with these words: "Therefore, since we are surrounded by such a great cloud of witnesses, let us throw off everything that hinders and the sin that so easily entangles, and let us run with perseverance the race marked out for us. Let us fix our eyes on Jesus, the author and perfecter of our faith, who for the joy set before him endured the cross, scorning its shame, and sat down at the right hand of the throne of God" (Hebrews 12:1-2).

MATURITY AS A PROCESS

Maturity is always a process. It takes at least fifty days for a sunflower's round smiling face to burst forth from the tiny seed planted in the warm moist earth. An apple seed can take up to ten years to produce ripe delicious apples on a crisp fall day. It takes nine months of life in the womb before a baby is ready for birth. An infant doesn't mature into an adult without first going through childhood and adolescence.

Spiritual maturity, like physical and emotional maturity, is a process that takes place over many years. We need not become discouraged or impatient with the process, because it is just that: a *process*. We will never reach the end until we die. I'm reminded of the children's story of the tortoise and the hare. The hare ran as fast as he could but didn't finish the race. The tortoise plodded along ever so faithfully and eventually crossed the finish line. Maturity comes by faithfully applying what we know to be true, day in and day out.

A child learns to walk before she can run. She will learn to skip and run before she can ice skate. She learns to skate well before she tries to jump on her skates. She learns to do a single jump before she tries a double jump, and so on. If at any time in our journey toward maturity we stop learning or practicing, we'll lose ground. As we walk in faithful obedience in the little things, we develop the character to handle the bigger things. The unfolding result is a life that is effective and productive in our knowledge of Christ, and we will receive a rich welcome into the eternal kingdom (2 Peter 1:5-11).

Fénelon says, "We must bear with ourselves patiently, without flattering ourselves, and we must continually subject ourselves to all that can overcome our natural inclinations and our inner dislikes, so that we may become more adaptable to the impressions of divine grace in living out the gospel.

"This work, however, must be peaceful and untroubled. It must even be moderate, and we must not attempt to do all the work in a single day. We must try to reason little and to do much. If we do not take care, our whole life may be passed in reasoning, and we shall require a second life to practice! We run the risk of believing we have advanced in proportion to our understanding of perfection"[2]—which only stokes the fire of our own pride.

The TRUTH Principle shows us how to apply God's truth to our life and establish it in our heart as well as in our mind so that our behavior reflects it. This is the pathway of maturity and growth.

TIME FOR REFLECTION

1. As you have become more familiar with applying the TRUTH Principle to particular incidents in your life, begin to look for broader themes of idolatry that keep you stuck in repetitive patterns of sin and immaturity. Look over the charts on the desires and fears of the heart. See if you notice any themes in your own life that may result in negative personality traits or behavioral habits that need to change. Instead of focusing on the habit, begin to pray about the idols of your heart and make a conscious decision to turn away from them. As you willingly yield up your loves and fears to God, continue to remind yourself of his love for you. Only as we grow in our love for God do we grow in our obedience to him.

2. Ask yourself the question, "Is it the desire of my heart to please God?" Our heart has many desires. If our chief desire is not to please God but to please ourselves, then we will never become the person God has made us to be. Pray and ask God to change your heart's desire

from wanting to please yourself to desiring to please him more than anything else.

3. Consider joining a small group where God's Word is actively taught and personally applied. God never intended for us to mature in isolation. He provided families to nurture the physical, emotional, and spiritual maturity of children. He also provided the family of God (the church) to nurture believers in continuous growth and maturity.

CHAPTER NINE

DISCIPLINES OF THE HEART

TRAINING OURSELVES IN THE WAYS OF GOD

*Whatever you have learned or received or heard from me,
or seen in me—put it into practice.*

PHILIPPIANS 4:9

My daughter, Amanda, plays the piano. She has been taking lessons for over ten years and is quite an accomplished pianist. Watching her develop this talent has taught me much about growth and maturity in my Christian life. When she was only five years old, she wanted to play the piano. She plunked around a bit but didn't really know what she was doing. I arranged for her to have short, fifteen-minute lessons to see if she would like it. From this small start, she has progressed over the years into long private lessons, with hours and hours of practicing scales, finger exercises, and piano compositions. Group activities that deal with music appreciation, music theory, performances, and competitions have also been a part of this training.

At times Amanda didn't feel like practicing. In fact, some years she felt like quitting. It would have been easier on all of us, but as her mother, I wouldn't let her. I knew how important it would be for her to develop the gift God gave her. She has stuck with it, and all these disciplines have become a way of life that Amanda regularly devotes herself to in order to fully mature in her ability as a musician.

Many of us enjoy watching sporting events on television. I especially love watching the Olympics, where top athletes from around the world compete to win the gold medal. What starts out as a dream for those young athletes becomes a potential reality only through years of disciplined practice, by which they train their bodies to respond to the best of their abilities.

The apostle Paul also speaks of training in order to win a prize. In 1 Corinthians 9:25 he says, "Everyone who competes in the games goes into strict training. They do it to get a crown that will not last; but we do it to get a crown that will last forever." He tells Timothy, "Have nothing to do with godless myths and old wives' tales; rather, train yourself to be godly" (1 Timothy 4:7).

Godliness is simply the nature of God within us. Although it is only through God's Spirit that we can have a changed heart, the Scriptures teach that we are to die to our old self and to discipline and train our new self to be like Jesus. We do this to be obedient, submissive, and pliant to his Spirit, just as Jesus' nature was obedient, submissive, and pliant to God the Father.

For the Christian, there are no shortcuts to developing the nature of God within. There is no magic prayer, no special verse, no healing touch. Just as an athlete or a musician develops his or her fullest potential through years and years of faithful training and practice, it is through a process of devoting our whole self through careful practice and training that we develop the nature of Christ within. A disciplined life doesn't come about by deciding; it comes about through practice.

Ideally, our heart's response to who God is and what he has done is repentance, not only in our heart but also in our habits. If we want to really grow up into full maturity as Christ did, we will need to do what Christ did.

When Gina (chapter 8) came into counseling with clinical depression and low self-esteem, she struggled with many difficulties in her life that could be summed up as a lack of self-discipline and self-control. Initially Gina wanted to grow as a Christian, but she didn't want to put in the training necessary to teach herself to respond to the Spirit's control. At the beginning, she wanted it to be easy.

Musicians and athletes understand that they will never reach their potential without hard work. Somehow as Christians we naively think that we can develop our new nature without such disciplined training. Oswald Chambers says that our "warfare is not against sin; we can never fight against sin: Jesus Christ deals with sin in Redemption. The conflict," he says, "is along the line of turning our natural life into a spiritual life, and this is never done easily, nor does God intend it to be done easily. It is done only by a series of moral choices. God does not make us holy in the sense of character; He makes us holy in the sense of innocence, and we have to turn that innocence into holy character by a series of moral choices. These choices are continually in antagonism to the entrenchments of our natural life, the things which erect themselves as ramparts against the knowledge of God."[1]

As Christians, we can have all the desire in the world to become more like Jesus, but having a desire is only the first step. Many of us desire to save money for retirement but have no discipline to make that desire a reality. Many of us want good marriages but do not take the time and effort required to communicate and relate effectively with our spouse. I can want to run a marathon until the day I die, but I will never be able to get my body to run a marathon, or even to run two miles in a row, unless I train my body to perform at the level my will desires. Most of us will never be top athletes or concert musicians, but in Christ our fullest potential is to develop the nature of Christ within so that our life glorifies God. Jesus told us that "everyone who hears these words of mine and puts them into practice is like a wise man who built his house on the rock" (Matthew 7:24).

A Native American elder once described his own inner struggle in this way: "Inside of me there are two dogs. One of the dogs is mean and evil. The other dog is good. The mean dog fights the good dog all the time." When asked which dog wins, he reflected for a moment and replied, "The one I feed the most."

Which nature do you feed the most? Is it your sinful nature with its corrupt desires, sinful ways of thinking, and natural disobedience toward the ways of God? Or is it your new nature, Christ in you? Our nature determines our appetites, our behaviors, and our associations.

A squirrel has a squirrel's nature, eats nuts, climbs trees, and frolics with other squirrels. A squirrel doesn't hang out with frogs or swim in a pond. It doesn't have the nature to do so. Our human nature does not desire the things of God. It is bent on serving our flesh and is corrupt and sinful. But if we are born of God, we also have a new nature, God's nature. He gives us new appetites, new desires for different behaviors, and different associations.

Paul warns us in Romans 13 not to think about ways to gratify the desires of our sinful nature. Instead he tells us to set our hearts and minds on things above and to put to death whatever belongs to our earthly nature (Colossians 3).

WHAT IS DISCIPLINE?

No one has to teach us to indulge our flesh. That comes quite naturally. I smell chocolate-chip cookies baking, and I eat one—or a couple. When I feel tired, I want to go to bed, even if I have important work to do. I see something I like, and I want to buy it, even if I was saving my money for something else. It is only through self-discipline that I don't give in to my immediate desires and learn to wait for something I want even more. In general, discipline is a tool that helps us achieve our goals in life. Without the tool of self-discipline our goals will only be desires, wishes that will never become realities. Self-discipline makes it possible to achieve our goals through the practice of restraining our fleshly impulses, desires, and longings and taming them for a purpose higher than immediate gratification.

Sadly, many people have not learned to be self-disciplined. Some find that their finances are a mess because they can't control impulse spending. Others struggle with bodies that are unhealthy because of poor eating habits, alcohol abuse, or other lifestyles that indulge cravings. Personal relationships are distant or rife with conflict because some people haven't learned to control their tongue or their temper. These problems afflict believers and nonbelievers alike. However, for the Christian it is not enough to be self-controlled; we must also yield ourselves to the Holy Spirit's control. Christian discipline is a process of learning to deny our fleshly nature and submit our thoughts, our emotions, our imagination, our will, our behaviors, and our desires to the renewing influence of the Holy Spirit.

SPIRITUAL DISCIPLINES

In his book *The Spirit of Discipline,* Dallas Willard describes spiritual disciplines as "time-tested activities consciously undertaken by us as new men or women to allow our spirit ever-increasing sway over our embodied selves. They help by assisting the ways of God's Kingdom to take the place of the habits of sin embedded in our bodies."[2]

When the apostle Paul tells us in Ephesians 4 to put off our former manner of life and to put on the new man, he is talking about putting off our ingrained, habitual behaviors that flow out of our sinful natures. We are creatures of habit. This is a good thing; God has made us that way. However, we have all developed wrong and sinful habits of responding, thinking, feeling, acting, believing, interpreting life, and expressing ourselves that need to be changed if we are to manifest our new nature in our bodies.

Our body expresses what is inside our heart. That is why the apostle Paul tells us to present our body as a living sacrifice as a means of worshiping God (Romans 12:1). Our body is the temple of God. Therefore, we need to train our body—our mind, our tongue, our hands, our eyes, our ears, every other part of our flesh—to respond to God in faithful obedience. It is through this training that we learn to allow him to use our bodies to express his nature to the world.

Jesus said that "the spirit is willing, but the body is weak" (Matthew 26:41). This expresses the cry of many Christians who try to put off their sinful ways but find themselves struggling in the same sinful patterns over and over. Jesus told these people to "watch and pray." Watchfulness and prayer are activities that we can learn to do better and better so that our flesh will respond to the dictates of the Spirit. I may want my hands to play the piano or paint a picture. My mind may desire to memorize scriptures or learn to play chess. But if I don't engage in concerted and faithful practice that leads my body to respond to what my spirit desires, I will never be able to accomplish these goals. The spiritual disciplines are methods by which we can make our spiritual nature stronger, more toned, and more faithful so that our whole body will respond and submit to the will of God.

Spiritual disciplines aren't sacred. They are mere steppingstones to a more faithful practice of our heartfelt beliefs. "They teach us an inner posture of not having to have our way, which relieves us of one of our greatest burdens."[3] It's tempting to turn the disciplines into rules that guarantee spiritual maturity. But this would be a grave error that would feed our pride and prompt us to think we can achieve spiritual maturity not by submitting our lives to God, but by doing certain activities. The spiritual disciplines represent a training regimen that arises from our love for God, not out of a desire to earn favor with him. The disciplines don't help us achieve righteousness, but they do help us to live righteously. Spiritual disciplines, when faithfully practiced, will lead us to greater intimacy with God and to a greater ability to love and obey him with all our heart, mind, strength, and will.

Just as a musician regularly practices his scales to prepare for a performance or a gymnast practices her routine before a competition, practicing spiritual disciplines helps us prepare to live effectively for God. I'd like to share some of the specific spiritual disciplines that help strengthen our new nature. Remember, the disciplines are not magic formulas for spiritual maturity. They are a regimen that deepens our trust in and dependence upon God. They strengthen us to stand when the storms of life hit, and not to be overcome when our flesh is just trying to get the better of us.

WORSHIP

In the Scriptures, each time a believer encountered God, that believer fell on his or her face in worship. Since we will spend eternity worshiping God, it seems to me that there is much benefit in disciplining ourselves to practice it more regularly and faithfully while we are still here.

During a short winter retreat to the ocean, God impressed me with a picture of his glory. I was sitting in front of a large picture window, gazing out to the ocean. The sun, newly risen, glistened on the water. Its reflection was so bright I had to bow my head to shield my eyes from the glare. I wonder if that's how the Israelites felt when Moses came down from the mountain with his face aglow with the glory of the Lord. No man has seen God, as even his reflection is too great for us to look at.

Sometimes in my counseling practice I become overwhelmed with the wretchedness of humankind. I struggle with doubting God's sovereignty and his love. It appears that the evil one is in charge, and I am tempted to believe the lie that God is not good. Worship, both private and corporate, reminds me that there is a much bigger picture than I can grasp and that there is indeed a good and loving God in charge of the world. During worship I purposefully take my eyes off my circumstances and fix my eyes on Christ. It is in this place that my spirit is uplifted and calmed. I am reminded that I can rest in the knowledge and assurance that he is almighty God, omnipotent and omniscient, in control even when I don't understand.

The discipline of worship helps my spirit remember what is true—that I am a creature and that God is the Creator. When I get too big for my own good, or when the weight of the world is on my shoulders and I think (in my pride) that I have to carry it, entering the presence of God through worship reminds me of Paul's words in 2 Corinthians 1:21: "Now it is God who makes both us and you stand firm in Christ." Worship keeps me from losing sight of my goal—the reward of "Well done, my good and faithful servant." It also keeps me from becoming distracted by temporal delights and losing my way through life.

Worship can also be expressed through my body. For example, lifting my hands in praise or singing to God with my voice are ways I can yield my body to the truth that God is worthy of my time, attention, and praise. To worship God is to fix my gaze on the loveliness of Christ in such a way that my emotions become one with my faith and belief in God. At that point, worship becomes more than an intellectual acknowledgment; it becomes a heartfelt experience.

PRAYER

As I read through the Gospels, I am struck by the amount of time Jesus spent in prayer. If we are to be like Christ and do what he did in order to become our true self, prayer must be an important part of that process. Yet for many Christians, myself included, prayer is something that gets put on the back burner of life. In the past I didn't pray much, and when I did, my prayers mostly consisted of asking God to help me achieve goals and move obstacles out of my way. Often I fell asleep right in the middle of them—even when I prayed first thing in the morning.

Have you ever wondered why Jesus spent so much time in prayer? What did he pray about? Certainly he didn't need to tell God what was on his mind. What was Christ's purpose in prayer? Oswald Chambers says, "One of the great needs of the Christian life is to have a place where we deliberately attend to realities. That is the real meaning of prayer."[4] Jesus described himself as always doing what his Father told him to. Perhaps it was in prayer that Jesus listened for the Father's voice.

Prayer as a spiritual discipline guards our heart. Proverbs 4:23 says, "Above all else, guard your heart, for it is the wellspring of life." As we bring ourselves daily before God in prayer, the Holy Spirit brings our mind, our affections, our will, and our emotions into submission to truth and gives us his perspective of the spiritual reality that surrounds us.

As human beings, we live on the temporal plane. This is where we reside until we die. The faithful practice of prayer, however, keeps our hearts regularly tuned in to the spiritual reality, or *truth,* all around us. (See Diagram 9.1.)

The discipline of prayer helps transform our desires into God's desires. Prayer is the process by which our heart becomes one with the

Diagram 9.1

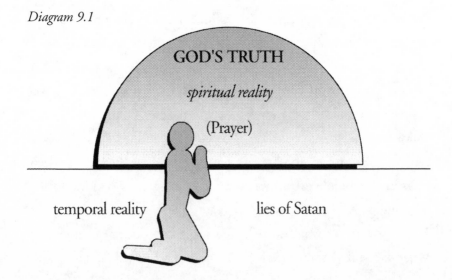

GOD'S TRUTH

spiritual reality

(Prayer)

temporal reality   lies of Satan

heart of God. We want what he wants, and when we don't know what is best, we know that his Spirit intercedes for us to bring about his perfect will.

As we practice the discipline of prayer, the process itself helps us die to our old self, which seeks to use God for our own agendas. "Do this for me." "Give me this." "Help me with that." Prayer is dying to *me* and living for *Thee.*

Mother Teresa said, "My secret is simple, I pray." She advised, "Love to pray. Feel often during the day the need for prayer and take trouble to pray. Prayer enlarges the heart until it is capable of containing God's gift of himself. Ask and seek and your heart will grow big enough to receive Him."[5] Prayer soaks your roots so deep in God's love, in his grace, in his point of view, that whatever happens on the topside of life will never injure your roots (Psalm 1:3).

Developing the discipline of prayer requires us to set aside specific time each day, or several times a day, to make our spirit aware of God's presence. By letting our heart and mind become more attuned to his Spirit, we remember that God's love is a real experience and not just a theological concept. Prayer teaches our mind to reflect upon life from God's perspective and allows his thoughts to become our thoughts.

STUDY AND MEDITATION

For a time in my Christian life I did not spend time with the Lord regularly. It just seemed impossible to find the time, and when I did, I found it rather boring! I know I'm not alone.

The discipline of study means that we take the time to learn at the Master's feet and then put what we have learned into practice. If we are not growing, it is because we haven't studied or aren't faithfully and habitually applying what we have learned. If I sit in a classroom, listen to the teacher, go home, and practice daily what he or she taught me, I will eventually master the concepts. But if I don't listen or don't pay close attention or don't go home and practice the concept, I may think I understand it, but I certainly won't have mastered its whys and hows.

The discipline of study involves the practical application—not just intellectual understanding—of spiritual truths. As a child, I learned my times tables fluently through repeated practice. Although I learned them years ago, I have never forgotten them. On the other hand, I studied French for two years in high school and two years in college. I memorized the vocabulary in order to pass the tests but never used it in real life. Do you think I can speak French? I remember a few vocabulary words, but I could never carry on even a basic conversation in French. The discipline of study requires me to take specific steps to apply what I learn to my life:

"Pay attention and listen to the sayings of the wise; apply your heart to what I teach" (Proverbs 22:17).

"Apply your heart to instruction and your ears to words of knowledge" (Proverbs 23:12).

"I applied my heart to what I observed and learned a lesson from what I saw" (Proverbs 24:32).

If study is a new concept for you, begin with whatever time you have. If you only have three minutes a day, start there. As you get to know God, you will want to devote more time to knowing him and meditating on his Word. My daughter started with fifteen-minute piano lessons; one-and-a-half-hour lessons would have overwhelmed her. As she matured as a pianist, however, fifteen minutes were no longer adequate for her to learn the more difficult compositions her teacher wanted her to play.

While studying the book of James, God showed my heart many things that I needed to change. First, I needed to practice joy in the midst of trials (James 1:2). That behavior contradicted my nature, which is to whine and complain when life is hard. Yet in order for me to develop the character of Christ, I must learn to endure trials with an inner joy.

I began learning to do this by practicing joy in the little irritants of everyday life. (If I couldn't do it in the little things, how could I expect to do it in the midst of a big trial?) Amanda has to practice her scales daily in order to keep her fingers limber for the more difficult pieces. Practicing joy in the small stuff of life keeps me "limber" and able to respond with greater joy than usual in the more difficult circumstances in life.

Dallas Willard says that the athlete "who expects to excel in the game without adequate exercise of his body is no more ridiculous than the Christian who hopes to be able to act in the manner of Christ when put to the test without the appropriate exercise in godly living."[6] It is not enough to stop doing wrong things as a Christian; we need to daily practice doing the right things. The opportunity for practice comes in the ordinary, everyday situations of life, not in the extra-ordinary "God moments." When those special moments happen, we want to be ready.

The discipline of meditation involves "an intense spiritual activity. It means bringing every bit of the mind into harness and concentrating its powers; it includes both deliberation and reflection."[7] Meditation focuses our intellect, reason, imagination, and will on a particular topic, story, verse, or image, allowing God to speak to our heart in specific ways. Meditation chews and swallows God's Word, digesting it until it nourishes the soul. The psalmist says, "I meditate on your precepts and consider your ways. I delight in your decrees; I will not neglect your word" (Psalm 119:15-16).

Once when reading the gospels I was struck by the story of those who brought their friends to Jesus for healing (Matthew 15:29-31). I began to meditate on that story. I imagined people bringing their sick friends before Jesus, filled with hope in this miracle man who healed people. Maybe their sick friends didn't want to come, maybe they were skeptical, yet the arms and legs of their friends carried them to Jesus when they could not or would not bring themselves. I asked myself how I could do this for my friends. How could I carry those that I knew were sick, crippled with fear, or blind with unbelief to Jesus? In prayer I used my imagination to carry my friends, those who were willing and those who were not, before Jesus for healing. The exercise revitalized my prayer life. Praying for my friends became more than saying words; it became dynamic action.

FASTING

If we think of fasting at all, most often we think of it in relation to praying and fasting intensely for a specific period of time in order to show God how serious we are about our prayer request. When our son, Ryan, needed minor surgery as a toddler to insert tubes in his ear, my husband and I fasted and prayed for him. God encourages us to participate in fasts for a variety of purposes (Matthew 6:16; Acts 13:2).

Fasting as a spiritual discipline is a regular practice of abstaining from food for the purpose of spiritual growth and strengthening. Fasting is a means by which our body learns to obey our will and God's Spirit (1 Corinthians 9:27). During fasting, our body cries out, "Feed me; I'm hungry." Fasting provides an opportunity to say no to our body's craving and to trust God in a deeper way to meet our needs.

Many of us live according to our fleshly appetites, and our will becomes subject to the cravings of our flesh. By teaching our flesh to obey the Holy Spirit no matter how much it wants something, our flesh will not be able to rule us. Fasting can be a regular spiritual discipline that prevents our flesh from leading us into places where God does not want us to go. First Thessalonians 4:4 says "that each of you should learn to control his own body in a way that is holy and honorable." Although Paul is speaking of controlling our bodies against sexual lust, many of us also find it hard to control our appetites when it comes to food. Our difficulty with self-denial and self-control becomes apparent when we fast. Hebrews 12:11 says, "No discipline seems pleasant at the time, but painful. Later on, however, it produces a harvest of righteousness and peace for those who have been trained by it."

You might also fast from things other than food that you recognize as having control over you. For example, a fast from sweets may become a time of growth for you as you abstain from things your flesh loves and put its cravings under a higher authority. Does the time you spend enjoying TV and movies outweigh the time your spend with the Lord or your family? Consider a fast from these pleasures, or perhaps a specific TV fast from sports or certain programs. Whatever holds your heart to the world and away from God will rule you. Fasting as a spiritual discipline helps us detach our heart from these things so that they no longer control our time or attention.

"Persons well used to fasting as a systematic practice will have a clear and constant sense of their resources in God. And that will help them endure deprivations of *all* kinds, even to the point of coping with them easily and cheerfully.... Fasting teaches temperance or self-control and therefore teaches moderation and restraint with regard to *all* our fundamental drives."[8]

SILENCE AND SOLITUDE

What would happen if you spent a day alone and didn't talk to anyone but God? We live in a world that continually bombards our senses. Televisions, radios, telephones, and computers are our constant companions. Rarely do we take time out of our demanding lives for quiet and solitude.

Yet God says, "Be still, and know that I am God" (Psalm 46:10). Many of us never allow ourselves to be still enough to hear the voice of God or to sit silently in his presence. Practicing the discipline of silence and solitude is difficult at first. Some people find the quiet frightening. We aren't used to being alone with our own thoughts. Yet carving out regular times in which to be quiet renews both our inner life and our outer life. Silence and solitude give us much needed space in our hectic, time-driven lives for prayer, personal worship, and meditation. It is in this space that we not only come to understand our own thoughts better, but we begin to grasp the mind of God.

For me, I find the best time for silence and solitude is first thing in the morning. There is something inherent in this time of day that readies my heart to be more quiet and open to God (Psalm 5:3). Once daily activities start in, it is much harder to carve out that quiet space. I would also encourage you to try half-day or full-day retreats where you can be totally alone with God. Some Christian retreat centers allow people to come in for a day just for this purpose. A day alone on the beach or in the mountains can also be a place of solitude and silence where God can more easily make himself known to you.

SIMPLICITY

For many of us, our struggle in the Christian life is not between the bad things and the good things, but between the good things and the best things. Simplicity is a discipline in detachment, in letting go of the things we love or the things we want so that our hearts do not become attached too deeply to anything but God. Sometimes our heart is attached to good things, but they hinder a deeper trust in God. Timothy said that "godliness with contentment is great gain" (1 Timothy 6:6). The apostle Paul said he had "learned the secret of being content in any and every situation" (Philippians 4:12). By practicing the discipline of simplicity, we can learn to be content with what God gives us and to willingly let go when he takes it away. Learning this takes time and practice.

For a long time I was attached to a good reputation. I wanted people to think well of me, and I became distraught when they didn't. I fretted, became overly hurt, and tried to bend over backward to please people who didn't want to be pleased. Simplicity meant I had to let go and trust God for what I needed. The result of detaching my heart from the love of a good name has brought me freedom—freedom not to have to defend myself, freedom to be who God wants me to be without worrying how people receive it. This has enabled me to attach my heart to how God sees me and to listen more carefully for his approval.

Inner simplicity leads to outer simplicity. Don't confuse the discipline of simplicity with self-denial or asceticism. Simplicity is simple trust in God and what he says. It involves acceptance in life and leads to being content with where we are and what God has given us to enjoy without holding it too tightly. As we practice the discipline of simplicity, we are not consumed with worry about getting more or losing what we have, whether that be in the realm of "stuff," relationships, or positions of stature and importance. When we complicate our lives, we become weary and distracted. Our heart can also be lured by and satisfied with good and nice things of the world, things that dull our appetites for the truly wonderful things of life, found only in fellowship with God.

For more reading on the subject of spiritual disciplines I recommend two books: Richard Foster's *Treasury of Christian Discipline* and Dallas Willard's *The Spirit of Discipline*.

THE REUNION

In contrast to the plain white envelope my invitation came in, my twenty-fifth high-school class reunion was to take place in a posh suburban country club outside of Chicago, Illinois. I wanted to go in the worst way, as I hadn't seen any of my classmates since my tenth-year reunion. But I had to prepare. Since it was a couple of months away, I had time to get my body into shape and shed the ten pounds that had accumulated around my hips and thighs. After all, I wanted to look good. I didn't want anyone whispering, "Wow, she's really looking shabby." You know what I mean.

I disciplined myself. I put myself on a regimen of low-fat food and no sweets, and I exercised four times a week. Sometimes I was tempted to indulge in pizza or ice cream, but I remained resolute, picturing myself fitting into that new outfit I had purchased a bit too snug. Nothing could distract me. I rearranged my busy schedule to accomplish my goals.

The reunion came and went and, I must admit, I didn't look too shabby. But God reminded me that a far more important reunion is coming soon, and I don't give it nearly as much thought or effort as my class reunion. Jesus will soon come to carry me home to heaven. There will be a reunion of eternal magnitude where everything that I have ever thought and done will be evaluated from an eternal perspective. What will perish in the furnace of his consuming fire? What will come forth as gold? Will I hear, "Well done, my good and faithful servant?" Do I commit as much disciplined focus to God's reunion as I did for my high-school reunion? Am I content to enter heaven spiritually fat and shabby?

At my reunion I wanted my former classmates to say good things about me. If only my eternal reunion were as pressing in my daily thoughts. I don't keep in the front of my mind the one whose perspective and approval ultimately matters the most. I don't discipline myself for the eternal reward. I want the goodies now, and I allow myself to get lazy and flabby. I forget that my eternal reunion is just around the corner.

Philippians 1:6 promises "that he who began a good work in you will carry it on to completion until the day of Christ Jesus." God is interested in restoring his image and nature in us. We can cooperate with God by training ourselves in his ways, or we can remain spiritually weak and shabby.

"It does not cost us anything to *want* to become mature, if we do not put forth any *effort* to become mature. We need to want God's maturity and perfection in our lives more than anything else."[9] The Lord asks, "For who is he who will devote himself to be close to me?" (Jeremiah 30:21). Will you?

TIME FOR REFLECTION

1. Read 2 Peter 1:1-11. In verse 5 Peter encourages us to "make every effort" to develop these character qualities. Use your imagination and picture the Holy Spirit as your personal trainer. What specific disciplines could you choose to work on to develop some of the qualities Peter describes? Make an action plan to begin practicing these qualities in your daily life.

2. Galatians 5:24 says, "Those who belong to Christ Jesus have crucified the sinful nature with its passions and desires." Begin to practice attachment and detachment exercises. For example, try a fast from the things that rob you of your relationship with God and with others you love. Can you detach from TV? Sports? Shopping? Working excessive hours? Instead, attach your heart to spiritual things through conversations with God, your spouse, and your family. Learn through this process to forsake or put down those things that you formerly loved and attach your heart to the things of God. Notice what a difference this practice makes in your daily interactions with others.

3. Begin to set aside a regular time for prayer and study of God's Word. Discipline yourself to do this each day, whether you feel like it or not. Your emotions are only one part of you. Exercise your will and decide to do it. In the process, open your heart wide to God. Remember that change comes about through habitual practice.

CHAPTER TEN

A NEW WAY OF LIFE

BECOMING OUR TRUE SELF IN CHRIST

*Be imitators of God, therefore, as dearly loved children
and live a life of love, just as Christ loved us.*

EPHESIANS 5:1-2

Over Thanksgiving my family flew home to Chicago to celebrate the
holiday with our relatives. I hadn't seen my brother's little boy for two
years. He was only four the last time I saw him, so I didn't expect him
to remember me. As we were reintroduced his mother said, "Clayton,
do you remember your Aunt Leslie?" He scrunched his eyebrows
together in a puzzled look and said, "No, but she looks just like Aunt
Patt." Patt is my younger sister. A couple of years ago she sent me a
birthday card joking that I was looking more and more like our
mother.

We all bear the image of our family heritage. I have my mother's
eyes and build. My son resembles his father. My daughter is Korean,
and her physical features are from her Asian heritage, but some of her
hand gestures and mannerisms resemble mine.

Not only does our appearance physically resemble that of other
family members, but in time we also begin to bear the image of the
kind of life we have lived. Gasper and Ruth were an elderly couple my

husband and I came to know early in our marriage. They were an inspiration to us because they wore on their wrinkled faces the lines of a happy marriage. Others come to have faces etched with worry or scored with bitterness. "As water reflects a face, so a man's heart reflects the man" (Proverbs 27:19). Ultimately our lives come to reflect the image of what is in our heart.

EVERY PERSON BEARS AN IMAGE

Dietrich Bonhoeffer, a young Lutheran pastor, was imprisoned and eventually martyred in Germany under Adolf Hitler's regime. In his classic book *The Cost of Discipleship* he writes, "Every man bears an image." And "Either man models himself on the god of his own invention, or the true living God moulds the human form into his image. There must be a complete transformation, a 'metamorphosis,' if man is to be restored to the image of God."[1] The good news of the gospel is that God not only redeems us, he restores us—to his image.

I have a friend who loves antique furniture. She has an eye that can spot treasures amid junk. Foraging through garage sales, auctions, and flea markets, she redeems pieces of furniture destined to be discarded by those of us less able to see its true value. But she doesn't stop there. After she redeems the furniture, she sets about restoring its original beauty. She starts with a thorough cleansing. She removes dirt, soot, debris, and old paint that has accumulated through years of neglect. Then she painstakingly fills in the cracks, polishes the hardware, sands, waxes, and rubs and rubs until the warm, rich patina of the wood is restored. She brings forth its true image, the original beauty and design that had been disguised by neglect, damage, and false coverings.

Sin, both our own and the sin of others against us, has tarnished our original design as God's image bearer. Our best human efforts fall short of God's original plan. Yet in his sovereign grace, God not only offers to forgive our sins, he desires to restore us so we might participate in his divine nature (2 Peter 1:4). Our destiny as human beings is to reflect God's image in our human body (2 Corinthians 4:10-11). Yet many of us settle for far less than God intends.

A poignant line in the movie *You've Got Mail* hit me like a bolt of lightning when I first heard it. Tom Hanks writes to Meg Ryan, "Have you ever felt like you've become the worst possible version of yourself?" When we remain immature and sinful, which *is* our natural self (Scripture defines it as the old man), we *are* the worst possible version of ourselves. We bear the image of the god of this world. God wants to restore his image and his nature in us. As we walk through the steps of the TRUTH Principle, God doesn't change us into another person. Rather, he changes us so that we become the best possible version of ourselves, the version he originally created us to be—like Jesus (Romans 8:29).

As believers we have a new Spirit, the Holy Spirit living in us, but the stuff of life continues to prevent us from brightly reflecting his image. Much like a dirty window, our soul is covered with soot and sludge. Some is there due to our own choices. Other debris on the window of our soul has been smeared there by those who have injured us by sinning against us. The TRUTH Principle gives us a process by which we can see the sin in our heart and life more clearly. Through it, God's Word and Spirit teach us *how* to clear away the debris, the habits of sin, our false loves, the idols of our heart, and the deep wounds inflicted by others. God's desire is to remove anything and everything that prevents his image from shining forth through us.

The apostle Paul tells us that we are to be imitators of Christ and to live a life of love (Ephesians 5:1). As we mature, we are to look more and more like Jesus. We are his image bearers. Whose image do you bear?

The apostle John tells us that "God is light; in him there is no darkness at all. If we claim to have fellowship with him yet walk in the darkness, we lie and do not live by the truth" (1 John 1:5-6). Where do you walk most regularly? (See Chart 10.1.) All of us, at times, slip into the darker path of life. Our flesh gets the best of us, and we stumble into selfishness, pride, or the like. When this occurs, do we recognize what is happening and respond to God with a repentant heart? Do we submit to God's right to correct and rule us, or do we stay in the dark? As new creations in Christ, God equips us by his Spirit to walk in the light. To do anything short of that is to rob ourselves of the opportunity to become the person he has designed us to be—a person who bears his image and glorifies him through our life—our *true* self.

Chart 10.1

Light	(Ephesians 5:8-15)	Darkness
truth		lies
love		hate/fear
hope		despair
humility		pride
faith		doubt
kindness		selfishness
joy		wrath
forgiveness		bitterness/resentment
peace		worry/anxiety
goodness		self-centeredness
self-control		self-indulgence

Don Barsuhn, now retired, was my former pastor. I remember a story he told of a special visit he had with an unchurched family in the area. He took them some much needed groceries, talked for a while with the parents, played with the children, and prayed with them before leaving. Later, one of the parents called him. He had forgotten his hat. One of the children had found it and said, "Mommy, Mommy, Jesus forgot his hat!"

For those who will never step foot into a church, we are the only Bible they will ever read, the only Jesus they will ever see. Do we look like him?

DYING TO SELF

Dying to self is a phrase that used to trouble me. I wasn't quite sure what it meant or how to do it. Did it mean that I was to die to my thoughts, my feelings, my desires, and just go along with whatever anyone else thought or wanted? Did it mean that I was to have no personality, no individuality, nothing that made me distinct as a separate person from the body of Christ?

I don't believe that is what the Bible teaches when it speaks of dying to self. In order to become our true self in Christ, we must first recognize and deal with our false or old self. Each of us in our sinful nature has created a self that is contrary to God's best for us. *Giving up our false self* is the process of dying to self.

The apostle Paul scolded the Corinthian church for being too immature to receive solid food (1 Corinthians 3:2). Greater maturity involves harder tasks. In nature, change or growth often requires death. A seed must die before it can become a tree, and a caterpillar dies to itself before transforming into a beautiful butterfly. Likewise, spiritual growth in a Christian's life involves death—death of self. We have difficulty understanding this because we want to live and we don't want to die. But unless we are willing to die to our old self, God cannot bring forth our new self, created to be like Jesus.

Dying to self begins after a person has come to understand that she has a self to die to. Many people stay immature because they don't do the hard work involved in knowing who they are and what they want. Ashley came to counseling because she felt depressed. She didn't know why or when it started. When I inquired about Ashley's past, I found that Ashley was always a "good girl" and did whatever she was told. She never caused any waves, she never voiced her own opinion, and she never worked to develop her own sense of self. Ashley lived her life without ever reflecting upon who she was, how she felt, or why she was here. Ashley's passivity may look like dying to self, but you can't die to a self you don't know you have.

The TRUTH Principle can help someone like Ashley understand *herself* more fully. As Ashley looked at her responses to her trouble, she started to learn what she thinks, feels, and does in the midst of life's difficulties. She saw that she responded by withdrawing from people, afraid of making a mistake or of being wrong. She never risked developing her own opinions on things. The TRUTH Principle also helped her look for the desires of her heart. This step was crucial for Ashley. The biggest desire of her heart was to stay safe, to remain unknown so she could never get in trouble. This was her false self, not at all the woman God intended Ashley to be. Ashley needed to die to her false self in order to become her true self in Christ.

In contrast to those who have not spent enough time looking at themselves, there are many others who have spent too much time focusing on themselves. Don had it all. At forty years old he had finally arrived. He owned his own business, bought a new Mercedes convertible, and traveled around the world with his computer company. But for Don, deeper maturity would come only as he realized that there had to be more to life than finding and satisfying himself. We will fully mature only when we learn that we do not find life in ourselves or in our pursuits. As we acknowledge this truth, God moves us toward a greater depth of spiritual growth. We come to understand in a different way that self-discovery, self-satisfaction, self-actualization, or self-fulfillment are all booby prizes of life. We seek it, get it, and find it empty. Jesus tells us as much when he says, "Whoever finds his life will lose it, and whoever loses his life for my sake will find it" (Matthew 10:39).

For all of us, whether we have taken too little time understanding ourselves or have spent too much time pleasing ourselves, the TRUTH Principle draws our heart to these central questions: What do we love, and what do we worship? Often we will find that we have many legitimate desires, ones that are not sinful or wicked in themselves but perhaps have grown too important and have become idols of our heart. These idols reveal what we want the most in life and to what lengths we will go to have those desires satisfied. In uncovering our idols, we will need to face the truth about whether our well-being is dependent on satisfying those idols of our heart or is dependent on God. This awareness brings us to a crossroads of life—and the opportunity for growth. Will it be my way or God's way? This is the death of the false self. As we find that serving self is shallow and empty, we can begin to die to self and live for God.

As Christians we may forsake worldly pleasures and call that dying to self, but most of us will still demand interior pleasures. "God, if only you would make me feel better…feel loved…feel your presence, I would be able to serve or love you." When we require God to satisfy our restless or painful emotions, we seek God to satisfy our self, not to satisfy him. Our primary focus is on us and what we want. Even if our focus changes from satisfying ourselves outwardly to satisfying ourselves inwardly, it is still all about us, not about him.

God is worthy of our attention, thoughts, devotion, love, obedience, and worship, whether he gives us anything back or not. Dying to self means we realize that there is something far more significant to our life than making ourselves happy (Ephesians 1:12; 2:10). With that realization, we forsake the path of self-interest and we begin a journey of love. On love's path we learn that self-denial, not self-fulfillment, is the way. We begin to willingly accept whatever God offers us without needing him to explain it or clear it with us first. As children of God and as his image bearers, we still have desires, but in the exercise of love—whether the love for one another or the love for God—we may be asked to lay those desires down (Galatians 5:6; 1 John 4:7–5:5). In love's service we may be called to lay down the desire to be understood, the desire to be treated fairly, and the desire to have temporal happiness. We first learn to do this willingly, and as we deepen our love and trust in God, we find that we can do this gladly. Jesus said, "Greater love has no one than this, that he lay down his life for his friends" (John 15:13). What greater desire could we have than for life itself? Yet Jesus tells us that in the service of love, we may be called to lay down our very life. It is our pride that keeps us so attached to *our* ways and *our* desires. It is our inordinate self-love that keeps us from maturing because we want everything to be about us and not about God.

Dying to self means that we begin, day by day, to let go, to surrender and yield to God's authority in our life, to trust and obey him to meet the desires of our heart, to live our life where everything is about God—pleasing him, knowing him, enjoying him, and glorifying him—and not about us and our wants. In Galatians 2:20, Paul says, "I have been crucified with Christ and *I no longer live, but Christ lives in me.* The life I live in the body, I live by faith in the Son of God, who loved me and gave himself for me" (italics mine).

We will never be more fully our true self than when we fully abandon ourselves to God and die to our old self. "[Our] actions are never more authentic than when they are the Spirit's actions through [us]. [We are] never more genuinely human than when [we are] most godly. The more harmoniously God lives within [us], the more freely [we] live."[2]

LIVING FOR GOD

The book of Colossians is filled with God's guidance for us to mature through this transition of dying to self and living for God. Paul tells us to "set your hearts on things above, where Christ is seated at the right hand of God. Set your minds on things above, not on earthly things. For you died, and your life is now hidden with Christ in God" (Colossians 3:1-3).

Each step of the TRUTH Principle helps us take these instructions and work them through our everyday life. It teaches us how to set our heart and mind on God's agenda and not our own. It shows us how to repent of our false loves and to discipline our hearts according to the ways of God. Peter tells us to "be holy in all you do; for it is written: 'Be holy, because I am holy'" (1 Peter 1:15-16). How can we do this?

LIVE WHOLLY IN THE MOMENT

Most of us live looking ahead, wanting to be out of the moment we're in. Others live looking behind, always regretting or reliving the past. If we live looking behind us, second-guessing ourselves, regretting mistakes, or nursing past hurts, it hinders us from living in the present and experiencing life *now*. Neither can we fully participate in the moment we're in when we live anxiously dreading or expectantly hoping for the future to come: "When this happens, I will…" or "When this is over, then…" As we learn to live in the moments we are *in*, we can choose to live each moment for God. The TRUTH Principle begins this process by looking at the moment (our trouble) from God's perspective so that we might understand what God is up to *in* the moment (chapter 2). Jeanne Guyon advises, "What is abandonment? It is forgetting your past; it is leaving the future in His hands; it is devoting the present fully and completely to your Lord. Abandonment is being satisfied with the present moment, no matter what that moment contains. You are satisfied because you know that whatever that moment has, it contains—in that instant—God's eternal plan for you."[3]

BE HOLY IN THE MOMENT

One year Patt, my sister, decided she wanted a flower garden. However, she was not interested in doing any of the work involved in flower gardening. Instead, she went to the local craft store, bought lots and lots of silk flower bushes, and planted them in her soil and pots outside her home. People would drive by and admire her beautiful flowers that never seemed to wilt. She got a chuckle watching the startled faces of those who walked past her home for a closer look when they discovered that the flowers they were admiring weren't real. Sometimes in our Christian life, we want to look good to others but don't want to put forth the work involved in learning to live a life that pleases God. We want the confirmation from our Christian brothers and sisters that we're doing pretty well. We want them to admire the spiritual fruit in our lives. Unfortunately, we can never let them get too close or they will discover that we are fake and that we have no real roots.

Holiness is not the same as a life full of good works, or even necessarily one full of right living. Holiness comes out of a right relationship with God. "Holy holiness is a relational holiness—it is God's overwhelming presence in my life, causing me to want to do what He wills as He gives me the strength to do it, however imperfectly I may live it out."[4] True holiness recognizes our utter dependence upon God and his grace to live a life that pleases him.

What can we offer God that will please him the most? He needs nothing from us. He is pleased when we offer him our sins, our trust, our love, our will, and our hunger and thirst in every *moment* of our life. It pleases God when we acknowledge that we are incomplete without him, that we need him and him alone to be satisfied with life. "God is most glorified in us when we are most satisfied in him."[5] God is not delighted in our sacrifices, our discipline, or our efforts to do good works. God is delighted and glorified when we humbly recognize our need for his love, his grace, his forgiveness to live *each moment* of our life. He delights in our helplessness and dependence upon him.

A CHANGE OF HEART

A change of heart is God's work of redemption and restoration in a person's heart and life. "I will give you a new heart and put a new spirit in you; I will remove from you your heart of stone and give you a heart of flesh. And I will put my Spirit in you and move you to follow my decrees and be careful to keep my laws" (Ezekiel 36:26-27). A change of heart is about our relationship with God and how the union of his Spirit with our spirit works itself out in our life. Throughout this book I've emphasized that if we love God, we will obey him and that we only come to love him when we know his love for us. God changes us through the power of his Spirit that lives within us. Love moves our heart to obey him. Jesus came in love through the incarnation (John 3:16). In love he willingly and gladly laid down his life and went to the cross (Romans 5:8). His love redeems us; his love restores us. His love changes our heart from a heart of stone to a heart of flesh.

Linda, a former client of mine, has worked over the past two years to apply the steps of the TRUTH Principle to her life. She has given me permission to quote an excerpt from her journal describing this newfound experience of loving God. She writes:

I have been experiencing much joy in my life these days. Joy, peace, contentment. A lot of it stems, I believe, from the knowledge and assurance of God's love for me. It's an anchor for me. A refuge. I was singing and humming yesterday, like a young woman in love—and I suddenly realized that was exactly the case. I am in love with my Lord. I love Him and I love His ways. I love His righteousness. I have an acute awareness of the "right-ness" of His ways. And suddenly it is so very clear—crystal clear—that His ways are always and forever perfect and right, reliably good and pure. And I love that. It's like finding a long-lost missing and critical piece to a seemingly unsolvable puzzle. It's as if the Holy Spirit has been persevering, consistently and persistently teaching me new thought patterns, new ways of looking at people and situations. New ways of interpreting, reacting, and responding to things. It's so wonderful when I "catch on." It's so wonderful to respond to something as He would desire me to. It's truly a "born-again" experience, as if I've passed into "the other side" from death to life in a practical, applied sense. I feel as if for the first time in my life, even for the first time in my born-again life, I am finally experiencing that "living water" that Jesus described to the Samaritan woman at the well…and I can testify that it does constantly refresh you. And although I'm not left thirsting, I continue to thirst for more because it's too good to stop. It's my lifeline, so to speak, the Holy Spirit, God's Word, both absolutely delicious to my spiritual cravings and my spiritual appetite.

Ultimately a change of heart grows out of a heart that is grafted into the heart of God. Jesus tells us that he is the vine and we are the branches (John 15:5). We are to abide in him and he in us. In this union, a transforming and powerful change occurs. In nature, the ability of a tree to bear fruit has nothing to do with its branches, and everything to do with the health of the roots and the vine. "When we look at a branch bearing fruit we would never say, 'Wow, look at the effort of that branch! It must be working hard to produce that fruit.' The branch is able to bear the fruit because it is attached to the vine, not because of its effort."[6] When we abide in Christ and he abides in us, spiritual fruit will be the natural outgrowth of that union.

The TRUTH Principle is a tool we can use to continuously draw our mind, our emotions, and our will back to the greatest commandments God gives us. Do we love the Lord our God with all our heart, with all our mind, with all our strength, and with all our will? Do we love our neighbor as ourselves (Mark 12:28-31)? If not, what is standing in the way? This process, living it day in and day out, is the crux of Christian maturity.

When will we reach maturity? When our highest aim is to serve him. When our greatest joy is to please him and our deepest desire is to know him. Our heart is being transformed each day as we allow the love and truth of God—who he is and what he says—to penetrate us so completely that we remain in him and he remains in us. As we grow up in Christ, we will find an increasing freedom to be our true self, the self that God has created us to be. For he promises, "you will know the truth, and the truth will set you free" (John 8:32).

TIME FOR REFLECTION

1. Whose image do you bear? Do people see *Jesus* in you or do they just see *you* in you?

2. How have you understood *dying to self* in your Christian life? Are you willing to lay down your old self (the false self) in order for God to restore your true self in him?

3. Begin to live wholly in the moment. Stop focusing on past mistakes or hurts. Quit rushing to get out of the present moment you're in. Instead, look for what God is doing *in* the moment to help you become more like him.

NOTES

Chapter One: Rules Don't Change Us, Relationships Do

1. Warren Wiersbe, comp., *The Best of A. W. Tozer* (Grand Rapids: Baker, 1978), 56.

2. Oswald Chambers, *My Utmost for His Highest* (1935; reprint, Uhrichsville, Ohio: Barbour, 1963), 160.

3. Chambers, *My Utmost for His Highest*, 112.

4. In this and in all subsequent stories, I have altered names and details to protect client confidentiality.

5. Sandra Wilson, "The Sufficiency of Christ in Counseling," (speech at the American Association of Christian Counselors Conference, Philadelphia, March 1995).

6. Sinclair B. Ferguson, *A Heart for God* (Colorado Springs: NavPress, 1985), 24.

7. Gary Thomas, *Seeking the Face of God* (Nashville: Nelson, 1994), 61.

8. This was a common saying of Mother Teresa that originated with St. Thérèsa de Lisieux, "Little Flower of Jesus," as reported by the Sisters of Charity Convent, Bronx, New York.

9. Donna Bryson, "Mourners Seek Mother Teresa," *Allentown (Pa.) Morning Call,* 7 September 1997, sec. A, 3.

Chapter Two: Troubles and Trials

1. Scott Peck, *The Road Less Traveled* (New York: Simon & Schuster, 1978), 15.

2. This diagram is not original with me, but I have seen it in many teachings throughout the years and am unsure of its origin.

3. François Fénelon, *Christian Perfection*, trans. Mildred Whitney Stillman (Minneapolis: Bethany, 1975), 134.

4. Henry Blackaby and Claude V. King, *Experiencing God* (Nashville: Broadman & Holman, 1994), 38.

5. Arthur Bennett, ed., *The Valley of Vision: A Collection of Puritan Prayers and Devotions* (Carlisle, Pa.: The Banner of Truth Trust, 1975), 25. Used with permission.

6. This is the answer to the opening question of the Westminster Catechism.

7. Bodie Thoene, *Vienna Prelude* (Minneapolis: Bethany, 1989), 339.

8. Jerry Bridges, *Trusting God* (Colorado Springs: NavPress, 1988), 18.

9. Bennett, introduction to *The Valley of Vision*. Used with permission.

10. Oswald Chambers, *My Utmost for His Highest* (1935; reprint, Uhrichsville, Ohio: Barbour, 1963), 93.

Chapter Three: Our Response to Life's Troubles

1. Kenneth Barker, ed., *New International Bible* (Grand Rapids: Zondervan, 1995), 783.

2. Plato, *Apology*, 38a.

3. Warren Wiersbe, comp., *The Best of A. W. Tozer* (Grand Rapids: Baker Books, 1978), 43.

4. Thomas à Kempis, *Of the Imitation of Christ* (Springdale, Pa.: Whitaker House, 1981), 40.

Chapter Four: Underlying Idols of the Heart

1. Saint Augustine, *The Confessions of Saint Augustine* (Uhrichsville, Ohio: Barbour, 1984), 11.

2. *Merriam-Webster's Collegiate Dictionary,* 10th ed., s.v. "worship."

3. Oswald Chambers, *Biblical Psychology* (Grand Rapids: Discovery House, 1962), 196.

4. Oswald Chambers, *My Utmost for His Highest* (1935; reprint, Uhrichsville, Ohio: Barbour, 1963), 207.

5. François Fénelon, *Christian Perfection,* trans. Mildred Whitney Stillman (Minneapolis: Bethany, 1975), 166.

6. Eileen Egan and Kathleen Egan, *Prayertimes with Mother Teresa* (New York: Image Books, 1989), 134-5. Used with permission.

Chapter Five: Truth: The Mirror to Our Heart

1. Richard Lovelace, *Dynamics of Spiritual Life* (Downers Grove, Ill.: InterVarsity, 1979), 88.

2. Stephanie J. Dallam, "Dr. Richard Gardner: A Review of His Theories and Opinions on Atypical Sexuality, Pedophilia, and Treatment Issues," *Treating Abuse Today* 8, no. 1 (1998): 23.

3. John D. Hannah, "Insights into Pastoral Counseling from John Owen," in Charles H. Dyer and Roy B. Zuck, eds., *Integrity of Heart, Skillfulness of Hands* (Grand Rapids: Baker, 1994), 348.

4. Scott Peck, *The Road Less Traveled* (New York: Simon & Schuster, 1978), 58.

5. Susan Muto, *St. John of the Cross for Today: The Ascent* (Notre Dame, Ind.: Ave Marie Press, 1991), 40.

6. James Bryan Smith, *Embracing the Love of God* (San Francisco: Harper, 1995), 31.

7. Leanne Payne, *Restoring the Christian Soul* (Grand Rapids: Baker, 1991), 193.

8. Eileen Egan and Kathleen Egan, *Prayertimes with Mother Teresa* (New York: Image Books, 1985), 23.

9. Steven Covey, *The 7 Habits of Highly Effective People* (New York: Simon & Schuster, 1989), 30-1.

10. Oswald Chambers, *My Utmost for His Highest* (1935; reprint, Uhrichsville, Ohio: Barbour, 1963), 176.

11. François Fénelon, *Meditations on the Heart of God*, trans. Robert J. Edmonson (Brewster, Mass.: Paraclete Press, 1997), 24.

12. Terry W. Glaspey, *Pathway to the Heart of God* (Eugene, Ore.: Harvest House, 1998), 111.

13. Glaspey, *Pathway to the Heart of God*, 144-5.

Chapter Six: Our Heart's Response to God's Truth

1. François Fénelon, *Christian Perfection,* trans. Mildred Whitney Stillman (Minneapolis: Bethany, 1975), 186.

2. Adapted from Lynn Heitritter and Jeanette Vought, *Helping Victims of Sexual Abuse* (Minneapolis: Bethany, 1989), 132. Used by permission.

3. W. E. Vine, *Vine's Expository Dictionary of New Testament Words*, s.v. "metanoia."

4. Thomas Brooks, *Precious Remedies Against Satan's Devices* (Carlisle, Pa.: Banner of Truth Trust, 1997), 60-1.

5. François Fénelon, *Meditations on the Heart of God*, trans. Robert J. Edmonson (Brewster, Mass.: Paraclete Press, 1997), 142.

6. Mario Murillo, *The Dark Night of the Soul* (Danville, Calif.: Fresh Fire Communications, 1997), 46.

7. Teresa of Avila, *Interior Castles*, trans. and ed. E. Allison Peers (New York: Image Books, 1989), 154.

8. Jay E. Adams, *More Than Redemption: A Theology of Christian Counseling* (Phillipsburg, N.J.: Presbyterian and Reformed, 1979). Discussion under "Don't Apologize," 221-2.

Chapter Seven: Living to Please God

1. Sandra Wilson, "The Sufficiency of Christ in Counseling," (speech at the American Association of Christian Counselors Conference, Philadelphia, March 1995).

Chapter Eight: The Big Picture

1. Edward Welsh, *When God Is Small and People Are Big* (Phillipsburg, N.J.: Presbyterian and Reformed, 1997), 18.

2. François Fénelon, *Talking with God,* trans. Hal M. Helms (Brewster, Mass.: Paraclete Press, 1997), 23-4.

Chapter Nine: Disciplines of the Heart

1. Oswald Chambers, *My Utmost for His Highest* (1935; reprint, Uhrichsville, Ohio: Barbour, 1963), 185-6.

2. Dallas Willard, *The Spirit of the Disciplines* (San Francisco: Harper Collins, 1991), 86.

3. "Interview with Dallas Willard," *Discipleship Journal* (September/October 1998): 27.

4. Oswald Chambers, *Prayer: A Holy Occupation*, ed. Harry Verploegh (Grand Rapids: Discovery House, 1992), 60.

5. Eileen Egan and Kathleen Egan, *Prayertimes with Mother Teresa* (New York: Image Books, 1985), 9.

6. Willard, *The Spirit of the Disciplines,* 4-5.

7. Chambers, *Prayer: A Holy Occupation,* 126.

8. Willard, *The Spirit of the Disciplines,* 167.

9. François Fénelon, *Meditations on the Heart of God*, trans. Robert J. Edmonson (Brewster, Mass.: Paraclete Press, 1997), 70.

Chapter Ten: A New Way of Life

1. Dietrich Bonhoeffer, *The Cost of Discipleship* (New York: Simon & Schuster, 1995), 300.

2. James Houston, *The Transforming Power of Prayer* (Colorado Springs: NavPress, 1996), 216.

3. Jean Guyon, *Experiencing the Depth of God* (Goleta, Calif.: Christian Books, 1975), 35.

4. Gary Thomas, *Seeking the Face of God* (Nashville: Nelson, 1994), 75.

5. John Piper, *The Pleasures of God* (Portland, Ore.: Multnomah, 1991), 241.

6. James Bryan Smith, *Embracing the Love of God* (San Francisco: Harper & Row, 1995), 47.

ABOUT THE AUTHOR

Leslie Vernick is a licensed clinical social worker with a private counseling practice near Allentown, Pennsylvania. She received her masters degree in clinical social work from the University of Illinois and has completed postgraduate work in biblical counseling, cognitive therapy, and counseling strategies for those who have been abused and those who have abused others. She has served on the board of directors of the local Crisis Pregnancy Center and is currently on the advisory committee for REST Ministries, a division of BCM Ministries. She has been a guest lecturer at Alliance Biblical Seminary in the Philippines and has been a featured guest on local television as well as Family Radio.

Leslie and her husband, Howard, have been married twenty-five years and are the proud parents of two wonderful children, Ryan and Amanda.

Leslie is a popular speaker at conferences, women's retreats, and couples' retreats. She loves to encourage and motivate people to deepen their relationship with God and others. If you would like to schedule Leslie for a retreat or conference, contact her at 1-877-837-7931 or at LeslieVern@aol.com, or write to her at P.O. Box 784, Fogelsville, PA 18051-0784.

Printed in the United States
by Baker & Taylor Publisher Services